Shortchanged by Shortcuts?

44 SURPRISING WAYS PEOPLE
RIP THEMSELVES OFF
WHEN BUYING OR SELLING THEIR HOME

Aaron Hendon

Shortchanged by Shortcuts?

44 Surprising Ways People Rip Themselves Off When Buying or Selling Their Home

Published by: Rational Real Estate Professionals

Copyright © 2017 Rational Real Estate Professionals

Printed in the United States of America.

ISBN-13: 978-0692959534 (Custom Universal)

Cover design by ElfElm Publishing LLC

Cover image @blankerwahnsinn | unsplash.com

"This is the true joy in life, the being used for a purpose recognized by yourself as a mighty one; the being a force of nature instead of a feverish, selfish little clod of ailments and grievances complaining that the world will not devote itself to making you happy.

I am of the opinion that my life belongs to the whole community, and as long as I live it is my privilege to do for it whatever I can.

I want to be thoroughly used up when I die, for the harder I work the more I live. I rejoice in life for its own sake. Life is no 'brief candle' for me. It is a sort of splendid torch which I have got hold of for the moment, and I want to make it burn as brightly as possible before handing it on to future generations."

G.B. Shaw – Man and Superman

Contents

Introduction

"Just 'cause you're following a well-marked trail don't mean that whoever made it knew where they were goin'."

– Texas Bix Bender

Imagine a car driving down a quiet country road on a hot summer day. Without warning it gets a flat tire. After pulling over in front of a barn, the driver gets out, opens the trunk only to discover there's no jack. Thinking, "Where am I going to get a jack?" he recalls passing a service station a mile or so before getting the flat. This make for an easy decision. The solution is obvious – walk back and see if someone at the station can help.

Now imagine, shortly after he leaves to the gas station, another car, coming from the other direction, also gets a flat in front of the same barn (what are the odds?). Like the first driver, this driver also gets out to look for a jack, and guess what? She discovers that she too has no jack in the car (I know - what a coincidence). Now, this driver, thinks, "Hmmm, how am I going to lift the car, so I can change this tire?" Not knowing about the service station, and asking a slightly different question, she notices the barn. There she sees a hoist used to raise hay bales that might work for her. She drives the car over to the barn, uses the bale hoist to raise the car, changes her tire, and drives off before the other driver even gets to the service station.

In the first scenario, the driver, in his single-minded search for a jack, misses an opportunity right in front of him. His swift decision to walk back to the garage for the jack was made almost inevitable by what he already knew. Knowing there was a garage within walking distance dictated his action.

Not only have they asked different questions – "Where can I get a jack?" vs. "How can I lift the car?" – but what they each already knew shaped what they saw, their actions, and therefore their results.

For the first driver, his choice seemed to be logical. From his perspective, given the question that came to mind to ask and what he already knew, it was the rational choice. His knowledge of the existence of the gas station shaped and limited his ability to ask new questions in a way that was invisible to him. Despite it taking him longer, and possibly costing him a few bucks, he likely wound up with his tire changed. At the same time, it's important to note, that that he likely never saw there was a free, quicker alternative. In fact, he might have even been delighted with his ingenuity. He could have been so happy he told his friends about the whole experience, and if the garage was helpful, he probably recommended their services to others.

But as in so many things, the obvious, most used choices are not always the most efficient choices. The second driver, unaware of an easy-to-think-of alternative, focused on the end result she wanted – a way to change the tire. If she had a jack, she'd have used it, but she didn't. With no solution coming immediately to mind, she was forced to look at what was around her. Looking at the situation with new eyes allowed her to see a path that was cheaper and quicker than walking a couple of miles in the hot sun.

This is a useful metaphor for both how I've come to write this book and the situation most people find themselves in when buying or selling their homes.

The "service station" I passed on my way to writing this book has been educating people and helping them find hidden ways of getting what they want. Thanks to years as an entreprenuer and a public speaker/trainer, I "already know" we all use shortcuts that keep us from achieving maximum productivity, freedom and joy. I've spent most of my time employed either in postions of service or education, not real estate. My perspective on life pushes me toward looking to how I can help people see what they don't already see, the seeing of which will give them power to get what they want.

When I became a Realtor, it took me almost no time to realize that people had no idea what was happening in the background when they went to buy or sell their homes. The automatic mental shorcuts that essentially use people when they're buying or selling their homes were shockingly easy for me to see. And is often the case, the more sure the people I served were that they already knew what they were doing, the less likely they were to be looking for better ways to do it.

Not only do people ask the wrong questions, they do what they see others doing. The "service station" they pass is "that's the way my friend did it" or "that's the way I did it last time" or worse yet, "that's the way I've seen it done on TV." They already have an "easy answer" in their head, so they don't look for new solutions. Of course, they don't know they're doing this. They, like all of us, think they're being reasonable, logical and smart. They've no idea they're spending more money and time than is necessary. They've no idea they are leaving tens of thousands of dollars on the table. Given the information they have, they're making the obvious choice. And, unless the deal goes horribly wrong, they, like the guy who walked for an hour in the hot sun just to get a jack, feel like they got a good deal.

Existing solutions to unexamined questions make us blind to the possibility of better ways to handle any situation.

What follows is my case as to what I see are the common short-cuts people take when buying and selling their homes. I'll also lay out what you, as a consumer committed to operating in a way that will produce results beyond the predicatble, can do to think beyond those shortcuts.

Now, I realize cognitive biases (another way of saying mental shortcuts) are tricky things. First of all, by their nature, we don't think we have them. And even if we intellectually acknowledge having them, we rarely respond well to them being pointed out.

It takes a certain amount of courage and an unusual commitment to oneself to challenge your existing thinking. In picking up this book you've expressed an exciting willingness to look for your own biases. Good for you!

The working title for this book was, for a long time, *You're Doing it Wrong: Common Mistakes People Make When Buying or Selling Their Home and How to Avoid Them*. I dropped it because I felt it set the wrong tone. The truth is, whatever mistakes people make when buying or selling their homes are not their fault. If you've ever fallen into any of the pitfalls we're going to discuss, it's likely because your brain is wired to do it that way and you had little to say about it.

My intention is that this book gives you the power to look at your next real estate transaction in a new way. Looking from a new perspective will give you an opportunity to both find a Realtor you can trust and buy or sell your home with confidence and ease.

Having helped thousands of people discover and move past the limits of their automatic thinking makes it no less moving to me when one more person steps into that journey. Thank you for the faith and trust you're putting in me to read and apply this. If at any time you have questions you don't think I've answered, please use the contact information in the back of this book to reach out to me.

Onward!

Chapter One

You Are Not Rational

"When we remember we are all mad, the mysteries disappear and life stands explained."

– Mark Twain

I recently read *The Undoing Project,* Michael Lewis' homage to Nobel Prize-winning psychologist Danny Kahneman and his collaborator, the cognitive psychologist, Amos Tversky. I love Michael Lewis for his uncanny ability to make the opaque transparent, and to take what might otherwise be considered mundane, dull, minutia, and turn it into an articulate, suspenseful story.

His books often revolve around some big "reveal" – something obvious after he points it out, but completely hidden before. For me, the big "reveal" in *The Undoing Project,* was that the field of economics has held, as a fundamental principle, that markets, and therefore people (for what are markets if not large groups of people?) operate in a rational manner. I suppose on some level I knew this, yet I felt more than a little incredulous that anyone familiar with actual "people" would conclude they behaved rationally. Really? Do you know anyone who behaves rationally? (I mean, besides you of course.)

It's hard for me to imagine that there are people who believe, and are ready to argue, that human beings behave rationally.

Who thinks this? What evidence do they have? We all act in ways that are not in our own best interest (i.e., irrationally). We eat those things we know don't work for our bodies. We don't exercise when we know it would make a positive difference. We spend more than we earn and, consequently, we don't save enough for the future we'd like to have. Everybody does some version of these types of things.

Acting in a way that's counter to your own interest is irrational – a statement few would argue with, and therefore, the statement, "You are not rational," is not an indictment as much as it's a statement of fact. The sky is blue, water is wet, rocks are hard, and people are not rational. Who is arguing with this?

That said, it's also important to understand that humans are not randomly irrational. Unless we're mentally deficient in some way, we're not just winging it, flailing at our choices of how to act. We are, as the noted professor and speaker, Dan Ariely, points out in his book of the same name, predictably irrational.

The thrust of the work Kahneman and Tversky created (that gave rise to a more precise field of economics, aptly named, behavioral economics) is that human beings' behavior is constrained from making rational decisions by a predictable set of mental shortcuts. Kahneman and Tversky called these shortcuts, or rules of thumb, "heuristics" and proved, beyond any doubt, that when faced with a complex decision with an uncertain outcome, people will, without being aware, use certain heuristics to come up with an answer.

In cases where close enough is good enough, this works out for us. But we don't do it only in those cases. We do it everywhere. All the time. Even when it's not only unnecessary, but also at times, and in ways, that produce outcomes that are counter to our own interest.

Now, exactly what does this contention regarding human irrationality have to do with buying and selling your home? Am

I suggesting that when it comes to the single largest expense you will ever have, you'll likely behave irrationally?

Yes, I am.

Do I believe that you'll behave irrationally, that is, in a way counter to your own best interest when buying or selling something that is of greater consequence than any other purchase or sale you will ever make?

Yes. Yes, I do.

Do you think I'm overstating or over dramatizing the singular nature, the massive impact, the purchase or sale of your home has on your life? Consider this: Do you sit down every month, for 30 years, and write a check for any other purchase? Compared to your home, do you and your family have more physical and emotional contact with any other item? Is there something you own that is more expensive to buy, sell, and/or maintain?

I don't think I'm exaggerating when I say your home is the single most expensive, and most impactful, thing you will ever buy or sell. And I'm saying you did so (or are about to do so) irrationally, and you don't think you are.

A real estate transaction will likely be the single largest purchase in your life – a bad time to be irrational, yet as a Realtor, I've seen firsthand this irrationality cost people tens of thousands of dollars along with creating much unnecessary stress and regret.

It's one thing to operate irrationally in aspects of life that are, somewhat by their very nature, irrational (love, being a prime example). But it's quite another to do so in areas that can be so easily measured and gauged. This book is my attempt to help people examine what goes into both sides of the process, i.e., both outside themselves (how real estate agents, think and operate) and their own internal process (how buyers and sellers think and behave). I will also paint a picture of how these forces come together in a typical transaction. My hope is to give you a chance to choose a more rational course of action than you might otherwise.

I promise you that putting in the mental effort to explore these concepts will leave you empowered and enabled to get what you want out of your next real estate transaction, and that is the whole reason I chose to write this book.

Demanding More

I'm not so naive as to think I'm going to stop people from behaving irrationally. If that were my goal, I'd take on something more globally significant than real estate. No, we're irrational beings. We make bad judgments based on a myriad of input, thoughts, emotional states, moods, whims, etc. That's not going to change. It is my intention, however, that this book help people slow down in their real estate transactions long enough to examine what is happening in the process, and in their own thinking, thus avoiding some of the common pitfalls their mental shortcuts create.

Let me say now, this book is for people hungry to find their biases, the limits of their thinking, and to think about something in a new way. If you're someone who's satisfied with all that you know about both, how the process of buying and selling houses works, and how you work, then this is not for you. There's no point in going further if you're content with what you already know to be true.

I write this for anyone willing to create being dissatisfied – not merely open to new ideas – but actually willing to create a demand, a hunger, to take a fresh, new look at how they think and act about buying or selling their home.

Listen, if you're satisfied with the way things are, then you won't demand of yourself what it takes to discover something new. I had the thought to call this book *The Unexamined Real Estate Transaction Is Not Worth Doing* but thought it'd make me sound even more pretentious than I already do.

If you're interested in discovering something new about:
   a) Yourself (how you work),
   b) How the practical aspects of real estate transactions work, and
   c) How the two of these things conspire in ways I've seen cost people tens of thousands of dollars...
then this book is definitely for you.

The Structure

I've broken this book into three sections. First, we'll examine some common mental shortcuts that people use when faced with buying or selling a house. What are these shortcuts? Why, if unexamined, are they problematic? How do they shape your actions in general? Then we'll look at buying and selling as distinct activities. We'll examine the way these shortcuts and biases shape specific behavior for people buying and people selling.

In each case we'll be looking at what behavior, if adopted, would be more likely to produce a favorable outcome than the one derived from the shortcut.

My commitment is that you're left with everything you need, at every step. You'll be able to choose to hire, or to not hire, a Realtor in a rational way. You'll leave aware of what every step of your process consists of and can operate in a way that's in your best interest. I've created supplemental material that's accessible at www.rationalrealestate.pro and if at any time you have questions, please use the contact information that can be found there.

Before we jump into it, I want to be very clear about one piece of terminology. You'll notice I use both the terms "real estate agent" and "Realtor" interchangeably. This is for nothing more than brevity. They are distinct designations. While every Realtor is a real estate agent, not every real estate agent is a Realtor.

A Realtor is a real estate agent who's an active member of the National Association of Realtors (NAR), the largest trade association in the U.S. This doesn't automatically or necessarily translate to Realtors being better at handling your transaction than someone who is not a member of the NAR. I encourage you to apply what you learn in this book about interviewing and hiring any agent.

For ease of reading, and my writing, I'll use one or the other as I go and what I write applies to both designations equally.

Ready to go? Good. Me too.

Chapter Two

Shortcuts

"Things that look like shortcuts are actually detours (disguised as less work)."

– Seth Godin

What about these mental shortcuts? Where did they come from? And how do they cost you money, time, and peace of mind when buying/selling your home?

These shortcuts, these heuristics, are automatic. In other words, without being aware of why you're deciding this action or that action, your brain uses these shortcuts for processing the information available and arrives at a decision. That the process is automatic, unconscious, and in the background, is what defines it as a mental shortcut. We think we're thinking, but in reality, we're reacting mechanically.

This isn't a problem in and of itself. In fact, it's necessary. It'd be untenable to go through life having to calculate the actual risks and rewards of every possible situation. In many, if not most, areas of our lives, arriving at answers that are "close enough for jazz" works just fine. I don't need to know the actual, precise costs and benefits of, say, taking a specific route to work every day. I take the route I take, and am generally satisfied with it. I can live with the five minutes more or less that might be available if I were to choose a different route. Likewise, if one day, I see a piano being hoisted into a building by some sort of rope and pulley system (because obviously, I was also transported back in time to when pianos were hoisted by ropes and pulleys), I'd be likely to walk around it without needing to calculate the precise likelihood of it falling. I don't need to know the rope's tensile strength or the weight and strength of the person doing the hoisting. I'd make an instant judgment and step around the area. I've seen enough cartoons to know that ropes break, and while Wiley E. Coyote might shake himself back from a flattened state, such an outcome is less likely for me.

But what is actually happening when I make that snap judgment? What's the process my brain used to do that? If it wasn't based on facts (e.g., tensile strength), what was it based on?

For the purposes of this book, the question could be: Is what happens when we make such snap judgments always useful? Does it always lead us to the best possible outcome? When the impact of the wrong choice is the difference between a five-minute detour and possible death, it's a no-brainer, but what happens when the outcomes are less obvious?

In the case of buying and selling your home, what snap judgments are you using? Why do you pick one real estate agent over another? Where did the dollar value you placed on your home come from? Is it based on rational thought or arrived at by a mental shortcut?

There are hundreds, if not thousands, of variables in an ordinary real estate transaction – exactly the kind of situation that the process of natural selection encouraged, developed, and refined the heuristics or shortcuts we're talking about. Your brain was made to make these kinds of decisions in a snap. In life-or-death situations, when an instant answer is necessary, your brain does a great job. But real estate is not life or death and instant answers are not necessary. While there's a considerable amount of money and a good chunk of peace of mind at stake, it isn't life or death, and even in the fastest moving markets, you needn't be pressed into generating an instant answer.

These mental shortcuts have been exploited for years by masters of advertising and marketing, well before they were distinguished and studied. Their effects have been recognized and used to sell us everything from snake oil to our elected officials (a juxtaposition I couldn't resist using).

The mission of this book is to shed some light on these shortcuts. I'm out to raise some questions where none might exist for you now. What is going on in the ways you think (or don't think) before, during, and after buying or selling your home? And how might that thinking cost you time, money, and peace of mind?

As a disclaimer, let me make a few things clear. I've never taken a course in economics and the closest I came to a psychology class was failing Psych 101 in 1982. This was the year I won both Partier and Drinker of the Year at my fraternity – the first time anyone ever won both awards the same year. I could only be prouder of this accomplishment if I could remember any of what happened.

Let's just say that academia is not a strong suit for me and leave it at that, okay? This is not some treatise on behavioral economics. I'm not pretending what I'm saying is 100 percent technically accurate. I have no doubt true students of psychology and/or economic theory could point out inconsistencies and inaccuracies.

My point isn't to teach you behavioral economics as a theory. I'm a layman applying common economic theories, as I understand them, on a very specific, practical, and impactful scenario. A scenario almost all Americans will deal with and for which, in my personal experience, they are woefully unprepared.

I've done my research in good faith attempting to get at least close to making sense to someone familiar with these theories. I've written from my observations of how people actually behave when shopping for a real estate agent, a home, or putting their own home up for sale.

It's my hope that you, in seeing what's happening in your thinking, will be able to use this insight to alter your behavior and make more rational decisions in what is the single most expensive, and one of the most impactful, purchases or sales of your life. In other words, if these shortcuts are at the source of what brand of toothpaste or beer wind up in your cart the next time you're at the store, the impact on you is negligible. And be clear, there are, literally, billions of dollars being spent to make sure that these shortcuts *are* at play when you do fill your cart.

However, when these shortcuts cause you to lose the house of your dreams to another buyer, or when the sale of your home nets you $25,000 less than you could have gotten and takes you an extra 90 days to sell – well, that's a much bigger deal.

Specifically, the shortcuts we'll be looking at are known as: ***Representativeness, Availability, Prospect Theory, Confirmation Bias,*** and ***Anchoring***.

The way I have this broken out, for what I hope is ease of use, is to first look at each shortcut to create a little background and shore up your understanding. Then, depending whether your interest is in home buying or in home selling, you can reference the steps of those processes. I've dedicated a chapter for each phase of the process so as to empower you to know what to expect and what questions you could, and should, be asking.

I'll also be pointing out the common places where these short-cuts come into play and provide alternate ways to think about that step of the process, so you have a greater opportunity to produce the results you're looking for.

Let's get started!

Shortcut #1: Representativeness vs. Base Rate

Look at these two examples and tell me what you think:

1. Which of the following outcomes is more likely out of flipping a coin ten times (H=heads and T=tails):
   a) THTTHTHTTH or
   b) HHHHHHHHHH

2. Meet Tom. Tom is of high intelligence, although lacking in true creativity. He has a need for order and clarity, and for neat and tidy systems in which every detail finds its appropriate place. His writing is rather dull and mechanical, occasionally enlivened by somewhat corny puns and by flashes of imagination of the sci-fi type. He has a strong drive for competence. He seems to feel little sympathy for other people and does not enjoy interacting with others. Self-centered, he nonetheless has a deep moral sense.

   Which degree is Tom most likely studying for: engineering or social sciences/history?

The correct answers are:

1. The coin is as likely to be flipped in either pattern.
2. Tom is far more likely to be a social science major than an engineering major.

Surprised? If you came up with different answers, you were answering through a heuristic. Don't worry though, most people get these wrong. Why? Because we're horrible statisticians. Counter to the view we have of ourselves, we're lousy at predicting the actual probability of something occurring. Making this worse, when specific details are scattered into the data, we become less accurate in our judgments. In fact, often the more detailed the available data, the more likely someone is to use it to determine the answer, regardless of whether the information is relevant to the likelihood of the event happening.

Let's look only at the facts to arrive at answers that have a higher statistical probability.

1. Each individual coin flip always has a 50/50 chance of coming up heads or tails. Therefore, the chances of either pattern being flipped in that exact sequence are identical.

2. There are currently 17 times more social science/history majors enrolled in school than there are engineering majors. Therefore, regardless of what you know about Tom, he's statistically 17 times more likely to be a student of social science than engineering.

It's still hard to get sometimes. Look, if the question was changed and you knew Tom also loved historical novels, late night debates about political theory and enjoyed traveling to sites of famous battles, what would your answer have been? Suppose none of that information was available and all you knew was that Tom is 5'5" and weighs 140 lbs. What then? Suppose you knew Tom liked dogs, kids, New Age music, horoscopes, Marlboro Lights, and sushi?

The logic behind assuming that Tom is an engineer isn't based on facts. It's based on a story you constructed out of the information you had on hand. If you felt Tom was more likely to be enrolled as an engineer, you did so because of an image you have in your mind of what characteristics *represent* an engineering student.

Details matter, but not in the way you think they do. Having more information can lead you further from the probable answer if the information you have causes what you're looking at to fit into a specific *representative* mold. Your brain is a pattern-seeking machine. Its job is to look for patterns and fit the world around you into patterns that are familiar to you.

In the case of the coin flip, the first pattern looks more random, that is, it's more *representative* of the image you have in your mind of a random coin flip. That the odds of either pattern arising are identical is irrelevant in this logic. Known as the Gambler's Fallacy, it's another example of how, rather than dealing with the specific probabilities of something happening, we're more than satisfied with going by our "gut." We are, in fact, organized to do so.

We don't generally use statistical data when making decisions. We use data in the form of a story, data after it has been "patterned." Yet we operate as if our decisions are based not on a story but on the statistical likelihood of an event happening.

If you said Tom was an engineering student rather than a social sciences student, you were using your personal interpretation of the information you had. You used subjective characteristics rather than the fact that there are 17 times more people studying social sciences to make your decision. For many people, even if they have the numbers of students in each field at their disposal, they still rely on the way the information they have "patterns" itself into a story that *represents* what they picture as an engineering student.

This shortcut, identified by Kahneman and Tversky as the *Representative Heuristic*, has us substitute the pictures we hold in our mind in place of statistically accurate information. The pull of base rate (the statistical probability of something being more likely to be true) is far weaker than the *Representative Heuristic* in moving the needle in our decision making, yet most of us purport ourselves to be rational in our decision making. The truth is we're woefully unprepared to use the statistical likelihood of an event or outcome happening to make our decisions.

The *Representativeness Heuristic*, like all heuristics, is automatic, unseen, operating in the background, and has us make assumptions and often take actions that are counter to what reality says would be productive. The shortcut has us pretend, has us act as if, our answers are based on statistical probability and not our stories.

As we go forward, you'll have a chance to look at how this shortcut can impact everything from selecting the best Realtor to selecting the right home.

Shortcut #2: The Availability Heuristic

The term, first coined in 1973 by Kahneman and Tversky, suggests that things that come to mind easily are believed to be far more common, and more impactful, than things that take more effort to retrieve in our minds. Sort of like, if we can think of it, it must be important.

As an example of this shortcut at play, consider this experiment:

First, an extensive study of the English language determined the relative positions of where letters appear in words. People were then given a random piece of literature and asked to guess if the letter K more frequently appears as the first or third letter of the words in the selected text.

Without going back to count, think about this book and guess for yourself. Are there more words that start with K or more words with K as the third letter? How many more?

Most people guess there are twice as many words that start with K as have K in the third position. In reality, this is almost exactly backward. Overall, in the English language words with K as the third letter are roughly twice as common as words that start with K (Mayzner and Tresselt, 1965). This is true of this book as well.

So why would you think it's the other way around? Tversky and Kahneman suggested it's because it's easier to think of words that start with K than it is to think of words that have K as the third letter. That is, words with K as the first letter are more *available* in our minds, so we place more weight on them.

Another study in *availability* asked a group of subjects to share six examples of when they'd been assertive in life (most could think of six). Another group was asked for 12 examples, which few people could complete. Both groups were then asked to rate how assertive they were. The group that had been asked to recount just six occasions scored themselves higher because, it was interpreted, their *available* data had a greater proportion of being assertive. (Schwartz 1991)

Even fictitious things, if present (*available*) for us, can drive our behavior. I know I've been impacted by this shortcut when my wife has had dreams during which my behavior was less than, how shall we say, appropriate. Regardless of the fact this was a dream she had while I was asleep by her side, the memory of what I had "done" was *available* to her and the impact on our communication was very real. (It's cool now though; I apologized for the way I acted in her dream and we've agreed to move on.)

Availability is at the source of people being worried about rare, but vivid, events. It's why, when you see a car accident while driving, you adjust your driving even though conditions are the same as they were before seeing the accident.

It is the *Availability Heuristic* that has us live in fear of terrorism, homicide, or child abduction, and wind up spending energy and resources to avoid events that are rare but vivid. At the same time, asymptomatic diseases that are both common and deadly are ignored because they're not *available* in our ordinary thought.

Anything that keeps the idea or event stuck in our mind will impact its *availability* and thus unwittingly shape our judgments. The more recent the event, the more likely it is to shape our actions, which is why we can say that time heals all wounds. As memories fade, they become less *available*.

Vividness is a critical factor in *availability*. Psychologists have shown that when test subjects were told of a new disease that had recently been discovered, those taking the time to imagine their life with the disease estimated they were more likely to be infected than the group that was told about it but not asked to visualize their life with the disease.

These heuristics, these mental shortcuts, are part of our naturally selected inheritance. It's suspected that having negative outcomes stay in our minds longer and more vividly than positive ones is a matter of survival. Most readers will have experienced some form of this shortcut firsthand. Fear of negative outcomes is a greater driver of action than desire for positive ones partly because negative outcomes are more *available* to us.

Here then, is a direct link here to our next heuristic – *Prospect Theory*.

Shortcut #3: Prospect Theory

The fact that avoiding loss is more important to people than attracting gains is not much of surprise. That it might be partially explained as a result of the *Availability Heuristic* makes it no less interesting to explore.

Prospect Theory shows us how we operate when faced with the choices of potential losses and gains… and, surprise surprise surprise, it's not rational!

According to *Prospect Theory*, first introduced by Kahneman and Tversky in 1979, regardless of the statistical likelihood of an outcome occurring, if it looks like the risk is high, we focus on potential losses, but when it looks like the risk is low, we switch to focusing on potential gains. Where we don't look is the statistical probabilities and then decide from there.

If you were offered a 95% chance of winning $10,000 or a 100% chance of winning $9,000, most people would choose the sure thing, even though statistically it's a worse deal.

However, if the prospects were reversed and you were told you had a 95% chance of losing $10,000 or a 100% chance of losing $9,000 most people would take the chance.

Prospect Theory dictates that when it comes to potential gains, people are, by default, risk adverse. When it comes to avoiding potential losses, however, people become, by default, risk seeking.

The fact that we will take greater risks to avoid losses is the heart of what's commonly known as loss aversion. Winning may make us happy but losing makes us miserable. We're much quicker to feel bad about loss than we would be to feel good about gain. There's a demonstrable asymmetry in our behavior when it comes to going for gains vs. avoiding losses. ***Prospect Theory*** calculates this roughly as a 2.5 times difference. In other words, experiments have shown we need to win $250 to feel as good as losing $100 makes us feel bad.

This shortcut has enormous implications in, among other things, our buying or selling our homes. For one thing, it makes no rational sense. When it comes to avoiding losses, you and I become irrationally risky. Our responses differ from statistically appropriate responses, creating more risk of loss not less. In other words, when faced with the risk of losing money, we tend to take actions that will increase the chance of losing more money.

Look at another experiment, conducted by noted behavioral economist, Dan Ariely:

- Salespeople were paid a commission to sell TVs.
- TV manufacturer "A" paid the commission up front. That is, salespeople were given the total possible commission for selling all of "A's" TVs before they had even sold a single one.

- TV manufacturer "B" paid the commission the normal way – after the sale.
- When a salesperson sold TV "B," they received $12 as commission, but, because they hadn't sold TV "A," they had to return $10 of the prepaid commission.
- While this still generated a net gain for the salesperson of $2, salespeople oversold TV "A." The pain of giving back $10 was greater than the pleasure of receiving $12.

The experiment above also illustrates the ***Endowment Effect***. We don't see gains or losses against absolute zero but against that which we already own. Once the salespeople were given the money by the manufacturer of TV "A," they considered it theirs. At that point, losing "their" money was more painful than the possibility of gaining someone else's, even when the amount of gain was bigger than the loss.

The ***Endowment Effect*** dictates that as soon as we own something, we start to look at life through the lens of potentially losing that thing. In a market situation, we tend to value more highly that which we own than the market is likely to value it (the market being those who do not own it). The flip side is that the market tends to value its possession (money to purchase what we own) more highly. Since we're averse to loss, it's no surprise that our perspective on valuing what we're selling is focused on the loss of what we have.

I'm certain you can begin to speculate how these shortcuts shape your decisions in buying or selling your home.

Shortcut #4: Confirmation Bias and the Backfire Effect

Confirmation Bias is the idea that we all seek, no matter how open-minded we consider ourselves to be, to find information that ***confirms*** what we already believe to be true. While science might be the game of arriving at the truth through pursuing evidence that contradicts the current hypothesis, our daily lives are full of anything but.

Consider this experiment Peter Wason conducted in the 1960s:

Look at this sequence of numbers: 2, 4, 6. Now determine the rule that governs the sequence. You can discover the rule by proposing your own number sets and receive a simple "yes" if it followed the rule or a "no" if it did not follow the rule. Once you're satisfied you've enough information, you can make a proposal for what the rule is.

What guesses would you make?

In the experiment, students came up with various hypotheses for what the rule could be, and once they did, they'd get fixated on it as the correct answer. In other words, they try to confirm their hypothesis rather than seek information to disprove it.

They'd see the sequence 2, 4, 6 and think, "Oh, that's a sequence of even numbers" and propose sequences like 4, 8, 12 or 100, 200, 300 or 6, 10, 18, and so on. Or they'd think, "It's a sequence that increases by 2 and propose sequences like 100, 102, 104 and 10, 12, 14, etc.

Now, all the sequences I just used all follow the rule. But neither "even numbers" nor "increase by 2s" is, in fact, the rule. In the experiment, once the students had come up with a rule in their mind, they continued to create more and more examples of sequences that fit their rule, even after they knew it wasn't the correct answer.

It's only by finding information that disproves or doesn't fit the existing hypothesis can you hope to discover the rule. But we don't do that. ***Confirmation Bias*** has us look for that which supports what we already believe. You can see this in the enormity of the political pundit industry (and the problems created by people speaking, and listening, only to those already thinking like they do).

Oh... so what was the rule in the experiment? I've shared a video of a version of the experiment here: www.rationalrealestate.pro/246 (Note: See the Resource section at the end of the book for convenient URL references.)

The Backfire Effect is like the insane brother of *Confirmation Bias*. Not only are we only looking for information that *confirms* and validates our already existing views, but if we do come across information that contradicts it, we tend to double down on what we already believe rather than change our belief to fit the new evidence.

History could not be clearer on this point. How was Galileo treated when presenting his support of Copernicus' theory that the earth was not the center of the universe? With a parade and as a hero? No, he was jailed for heresy. But, of course, you are not so closed-minded as to do something like that. You're rational. You're open to new ideas and welcome all points of view. Really? The evidence shows that, at least statistically speaking, you're not.

You only need watch your immediate reaction to what I just said – how open are you to my even suggesting you're not open?

There's a strong body of evidence that demonstrates correcting someone's misconception on any topic will increase their belief in the misconception, not decrease it. The more closely the topic is related to our personal sense of self, the more pronounced the *Backfire Effect* becomes. In other words, topics we consider trivial are not as impacted by this phenomenon as topics integral to who we consider ourselves to be.

A study conducted by researchers at Dartmouth College had people read an article containing a quote from President George W. Bush. In it was the assertion that tax cuts "helped increase revenue to the Treasury." In some of the versions of the article, this claim was then corrected with evidence that showed revenue to the Treasury actually declined for the three years following the tax cuts from $2 trillion in 2000 to $1.8 trillion in 2003 (a trillion here, a trillion there, pretty soon we're talking about real money, as they say).

Disturbing, at least to me, was that people describing themselves as conservatives were twice as likely to think the tax cuts generated more revenue when they were given the article with the contrary evidence as they were when they read the article without the evidence.

If for some reason, you read this and believe these types of results are particular to people of one political camp and not another, it might be best to consider you are, right now, at the effect of your own **Confirmation Bias**.

The upshot is that we're never as open to new ideas as we imagine. We have developed shortcuts that have us constrained when it comes to considering alternative points of view. We're limited by **Confirmation Bias**, we seek information that proves we're right, and then again, by the **Backfire Effect**, where evidence that's found proving us wrong is not simply ignored, it drives us further into our mistaken beliefs.

Whatever pre-existing ideas and beliefs you have about the home you are selling, or the market in which you are shopping, be clear that the impact of this shortcut looms large.

Shortcut #5: Anchoring

Anchoring describes our tendency to use the first piece of information offered as an "*anchor*" when making decisions. Think of buying a car – the first piece of information is the manufacturer's suggested retail price (MSRP). That number becomes the *anchor*. All negotiations now revolve around that number. When the salesman says, "Let me go back to my manager and see what I can do" and then comes back with a number that's lower than the MSRP, you've no choice but to think you're getting a deal.

This kind of makes sense. You'd have no way to really know what the car is worth or where to start the negotiation without some figure, so the MSRP serves a purpose. However, if you think **Anchoring** is limited to occasions that seem logical or useful, you'd be mistaken. Any random number will serve as an *anchor* and impact the amount you'll pay for something.

Consider this experiment conducted by Dan Ariely and Drazen Prelec in 2006 that Ariely reported in his book, *Predictably Irrational*. As professors at MIT, they had their students take part in an auction of sorts. For sale, they had a bottle of wine, a computer trackball, a textbook, etc.

The researchers asked the students how much they would pay for each one. However, before bidding, the students were asked to write the last two digits of their social security number on the top of the bidding sheet. Then next to each item, they were to take those digits and turn them into dollars and write them next to each item. (e.g., if I were taking the test, I would write 14 on top of my bidding sheet, as my social security number ends in 14, and then further down the page next to each item, I would write $14. If my son were doing this, he would write 82, and then $82 next to each item.)

Next, the students were asked how much they would actually pay for each item and to write it next to the dollar amount that came from their social security number.

What do you think happened? Clearly the social security number was a random, unrelated number. It couldn't possibly have anything to do with what people would pay, right? Let's face it: The students were well aware of what they were doing. They were clear about the lack of any correlation between the number they wrote on the page and the value of the items on which they were bidding.

The results? Students with social security numbers that ended between 80-99 were willing to pay, on average, 346% more for the items than the students with social security numbers with the last two digits between 00-20.

They could have used today's temperature, the score of a football game, or the number of angels you can fit on a pin as an *anchor*. The brain will not discriminate. It fixates on the first thing it sees and that becomes the *anchor*.

By the way, and important to note, this happens with more than money or numbers. The house you're in becomes an *anchor* in your mind that shapes and determines your thinking about your next house. You can become *anchored* to the past. The good ol' days, when gas was a dollar, what you paid for something last time, the way things used to be. All exist in our minds as *anchors*, creating comparisons that shape what we will and won't accept, how we will and won't behave.

Anchoring is related to something called the *Framing Effect*. Look at this example, also from Dan Ariely's book, *Predictably Irrational*:

Below are three actual subscription plans offered by Economist. com. Which would you choose?

1. Economist.com subscription – U.S. $59.00; one-year subscription to Economist.com; includes online access to all articles from *The Economist* since 1997.
2. Print subscription – U.S. $125.00; one-year subscription to the print edition of *The Economist*.
3. Print & web subscription – U.S. $125.00; one-year subscription to the print edition of *The Economist* and online access to all articles from *The Economist* since 1997.

What? Why would anyone choose the second option? The web and print for the same price as print only is a better deal. Why would they even bother adding the second option?

Mr. Ariely, determined to find out why they did bother, created an experiment in which he gave these three options to his MIT students. Of the 100 students queried, 16 chose option one and 84 chose option three. None took option two (and now we also know that MIT's admission process is okay).

He then offered a different set of options to a second group of 100 students. This time he only gave them two options:

1. Economist.com subscription – U.S. $59.00;
   one-year subscription to Economist.com; includes online access to all articles from *The Economist* since 1997.
2. Print & web subscription – U.S. $125.00; one-year subscription to the print edition of *The Economist* and online access to all articles from *The Economist* since 1997.

Now what happened? Without the middle, "useless" option, 68 students took the first, cheaper option and only 32 took the $125 plan.

What do you notice about this? By **framing** the plans and giving them a crazy option that nobody would take, *The Economist* stood to increase the sale of the more expensive plan by 263%.

There's no doubt that **Anchoring** and the **Framing Effect** save time, but do they provide more accuracy? Be wary that the more complex and rare the transaction, the more susceptible we may be to these shortcuts. Hint: buying or selling your home is both complex and rare.

Next Steps

You might have begun to speculate on your own how each of these heuristics, mental shortcuts, and cognitive biases might influence your next real estate transaction. As we go through each of the steps in a typical sale or purchase, I'll be pointing out ways in which I've seen these shape, and often misdirect, people into making choices that are not in their best interest.

Luckily, there is a body of evidence that shows being aware of these biases, that slowing down your thinking from making snap judgments and gut reactions, is sufficient to countermand them. As we go through each step, notice where else these shortcuts come into play. Bringing awareness to the thinking is more than half the battle.

Before we look at how these shortcuts impact your buying or selling your home, there's one more thing to examine. In the next chapter we will look at the way you look at the whole transaction and how a simple new viewpoint will reshape everything else.

Chapter Three

Mindset Matters

"No problem can be solved by the same consciousness that created it. We need to see the world anew."

– Albert Einstein

"Okay, what's the damage?" I asked.

I'm standing at the bus stop, cell phone in my hand, ear buds plugged in my ears. It's one of those dark-at-4:30 p.m. winter days Seattle is famous for, and it's cold enough for me to regret not having brought gloves. My auto mechanic, Andy, is on the other end of the line.

After weeks of avoiding the inevitable, I finally got him to look at my silver, 2001 VW Jetta wagon. I'd put off getting the clutch handled for so long, I couldn't drive it to him, so he's standing in my driveway.

"The clutch is about $1200. But since I need to pull the engine to get to it, and the age of this baby, I'd think you'd want me to replace the serpentine belt while I'm at it."

"Great... and how much more is that?" I ask, not convinced it was great at all.

"Well, it's about another $600 all in... and if you don't do it now, and it goes later, I'll need to pull the engine again and it'll be about double."

"Sure. Makes sense. Go for it." I say, and sigh the sigh of a man about to drop $1800 on a 16-year-old car.

And that's it. I'm getting a new clutch and a new serpentine belt.

Now, I know what a clutch is. I've rebuilt a few cars in my time. I like to think I have a good understanding of the basic mechanical features of a car. But I have only a vague wisp of an idea about what a serpentine belt might be. I assume it's something like a timing chain, but I wouldn't bet on it (and I'm a gambling man).

Ever been there? Ever been in a conversation where you're uncertain about something? It might have been something trivial and unrelated to you. Or, like me and my serpentine belt, it could be something important and costly. It's one of those times when you have a question you could ask, maybe even you'd like to ask, but you don't. Those times when you don't remember someone's name and are too embarrassed to ask, fall into this category. That ever happen to you?

What's probably obvious here is the concern stopping us is a fear of looking stupid. Nobody wants to look stupid. Doesn't matter who you talk to, or where you go, the pull to avoid looking stupid is universal and all pervasive. That is, we all automatically act in ways that will have us avoid looking foolish in the moment. Do we overcome this from time to time? Of course we do. But it's something we need to "overcome." What's automatic is avoiding looking stupid.

Let's go one level deeper here. What's the avoiding looking stupid about? Why do I fear asking about the serpentine belt would make me look stupid? Why would asking a forgotten name make you look stupid? What's the mechanism that has asking those types of questions trigger the fear of embarrassment?

Looking at these scenarios reveals a theme. In each case, you'll find there's the same assumption operating in the background. We may not be aware of this but it's there. If you listen to your own thoughts, you'll hear it. In every case in which you have a question to ask and aren't asking it, you think something like, "I'm already supposed to know the answer."

Asking any question when we're *supposed* to know the answer is bad news. It's a universal human phenomenon to have been laughed at as a child for not knowing the answer to some question. While we might think that was personal, that it only happened to us, it didn't. It happened to everyone. Nobody wants to look dumb, and there is no quicker way to look dumb than to ask questions we think we're supposed to know the answer to.

The end result is now, standing at the bus stop, talking to my mechanic about my serpentine belt, I need to suck it up, tell him to go ahead, and pray for the best.

Now my wife has no similar constraint. She doesn't have any hidden assumption that she's supposed to know anything about cars, so I know she's going to ask me about this new expense. This, I handle, in all my savviest glory, by researching it on Google before I get home (the moral equivalent of asking her to whisper me the name of that lady who just walked in to the party).

But what in the world does this have to do with buying or selling your home?

Consider, and I am asking you to stop and consider this, for real estate you think you're supposed to know how to do it. The background assumption most people have is, "I am supposed to know how this goes."

Look at the amount of freedom you have to ask questions. Do you understand what a title search is? Do you know what an escrow officer does? How do real estate agents get paid? How does an escalation clause work? What's the difference between the tax-assessed value and the appraisal? What happens after a seller receives your inspection response? Tell me everything you need to know about FIRPTA, or the CFPB, or lead-based paint and asbestos abatement... need I go on?

This brings up the other side of the hand. If you do know what these things are, you might be even more constrained. Knowing these things could leave you with "I already know about these things." The assumption that you *already know* is even more damaging to your ability to ask questions than the assumption that you're *supposed to know*. At least when you know you don't know something, you can overcome the barrier. People who "already know" something don't think they have a barrier to overcome. This was the case with driver #1 in the story I used in my introduction.

My point is, the damage is caused by not asking questions. The degree to which you're operating under the unspoken assumptions that you either a) are **supposed to know** how to do this, or b) **already know** how to do this, is the degree to which you'll have no power to ask the questions you need to ask.

Putting aside either of those assumptions is simple yet not always easy. First, you'll need to acknowledge which one is running your life. Are you a "**supposed to know**" person or are you an "**already know**" person. It's acknowledging this that will give you the freedom to create a new place from which to approach the process. By the way, it's possible to be either one at different times. It's the listening for which one you are now that's important.

There's one more hidden assumption I'd like to examine that shapes the buying or selling experience. "**Supposed to know**" and "**already know**" are assumptions you have about *yourself* that constrain your effectiveness. Let's look at one hidden assumption about *the situation* that also limits your effectiveness.

The National Association of Realtors reports that "Nearly seven in 10 buyers interviewed only one real estate agent during their home search." That number climbs to 72 percent for home sellers. This means that about 70 percent of the population will take the most expensive thing they own, the one thing they physically touch more than they touch any other thing, the thing that holds almost every key memory of their entire lives, and will put this multifaceted, complex, legal transaction in the hands of the first person who comes to mind, even if that person is a total stranger.

Wow.

What are the assumptions running in the background that would create this outcome? What world would you need to be living in to think that's a smart plan?

I can't answer for you, but I suspect it's something like, or at least includes, *"All real estate agents are the same, and/or I can't tell the difference between them."*

Either, or both, of those thoughts operating in the background would lead to an action called hiring the first person you meet. Those assumptions would give you permission, and perhaps confidence, in hiring your kid's soccer coach, or your nephew, or that nice guy you met at that open house 15 minutes ago, or hiring the person who offers the biggest discount.

If you start with the assumption that there's no real difference between agents, and even if there is, you couldn't find it anyway, then there's no point in interviewing a Realtor. Why bother? Everyone knows they're all the same and/or you can't tell (until later) if they're any good. Hey, seven out of ten people can't be wrong....

Except they are wrong. Even the littlest bit of rational thought immediately tells you all agents can't be the same. There's always good, bad, and average performing people in every profession. And, since they aren't all the same, what if you really could tell the difference? What if there was some way to discover who was most likely going to outperform the others? Would that interest you?

What happens if you put aside your default, automatic, "already there" assumptions? If all agents weren't all the same and you could freely ask questions, what questions might you ask? I have some thoughts about that I'll share in Chapter 6, but first let's follow this thinking a little further.

If you're going to give up your default, automatic assumptions, you're going to need to replace them with a different set of assumptions. In other words, you're always coming from some viewpoint, either a default, automatic view or one you intentionally create. Instead of coming from the view that you are "supposed to know" all this, or what you know is "all Realtors are the same," I'm suggesting coming from a different view will give you different results.

Here's one possible mindset you could adopt when buying/selling your home that might give you enough distance from those default assumptions. I'm asking you to take a moment and try relating to yourself in a particular way. See if you can picture yourself as the CEO of a business. Your business has assets somewhere north of half a million dollars (change this number to be consistent with the value of the home you are looking to buy or sell). And the business you're in has you out to either purchase or sell a particular commodity in a crowded market place.

I think that if you related to yourself as the boss, as the owner, as the CEO, and you related to the purchase/sale of your home as the business you were in, you'd naturally take different types of actions when it came time to find an expert to help with each step.

If you were the CEO, hiring a Realtor would be analogous to hiring a COO (Chief Operating Officer) or at least hiring a CMO (Chief Marketing Officer). Does every CEO hire a COO? Nope. But when they do, how many decide to hire the first COO they think of? Probably not a lot. What do CEOs do when looking for a COO? They ask around, they collect resumes, and they conduct interviews. And what do they look for during those interviews? They look for a track record and they determine if this is someone they're comfortable working with. Does the CEO look for specific performance results each potential candidate has had in the past? I bet they do.

Did you know you could do this before you hire a real estate agent? Did you know that you could ask any prospective real estate agent you think you might want to hire to show you their last 12 months of sales? You might not have had that thought before because your hidden assumptions have told you that's not even a question you could or should ask.

In fact, the assumptions have kept it from looking like you're hiring someone to represent you. I'm asserting it couldn't possibly look to the 70 percent of the population like they're hiring someone. What evidence do I have to back my assertion? Well, if it looked to them like they were hiring someone, they'd interview them. They'd use a specific, repeatable set of standard questions that uncover the interviewees' track records of past performance – because that's the action people take before hiring someone.

Changing the assumptions changes your actions, and changing your actions is the only thing that will change your results.

> **Key Point:** Does hiring someone with a track record of getting more money than average guarantee that you'll get more money for your home? Of course not. But expecting someone who has a track record of getting less money than average to, suddenly, get you the most for your home is pretty silly.

No matter what happens, in the context of being the CEO, you will be empowered to ask questions and make the calls that need to be made. The buck will stop with you.

Now, let's get into the information a CEO would need to run their business.

Section 1:

Real Estate Agents:
Why, How, and Who

Chapter Four:

To Hire or Not Hire

"In most cases being a good boss means hiring talented people and then getting out of their way."

– Tina Fey

Whether you're selling your home or out shopping for one, you'll need to decide if you want to hire representation or go it alone. Approximately 90 percent of all homes are sold using at least one real estate agent (if not two), so let's look at this as the first step regardless if you're a buyer or seller.

Despite my obvious bias toward using professional representation in a transaction as impactful and expensive as a home sale, I do from time to time, based on the individual case, recommend that people go it alone. However, because buying or selling a house is something people might do only few times in their lives, they better have a pretty good reason to DIY it.

Three shortcuts to watch for in your own decision-making process are *Availability, Prospect Theory,* and *Confirmation Bias*.

When you think of hiring an agent, are you an automatic "yes" or an automatic "no"? If you answer with an automatic, knee-jerk "yes" or "no," you might want to examine the source of it – is there a good or bad experience in your memory? Were you, or someone you know, burned by a bad agent and now that experience is influencing your response? Did you have success in the past going the For Sale By Owner (FSBO) route? Or maybe it's the opposite and someone shared a horror story of when they went out on their own?

It doesn't matter which way you're leaning, it's the automatic nature of the leaning that's important to examine.

Memories of good or bad experiences matter. It could be something that happened to you or something that someone told you about. If it winds up in your mind, it's now *available* to you and can shape your judgment. The more vivid the memory, the more impact this will have on your "gut" feelings about whether to hire an agent or not.

Be careful of taking on risk here. Because negative experiences are stored more vividly, they'll be more *available*. *Prospect Theory* dictates you'll become a risk taker when faced with the threat of loss. Even threats that exist only in the form of shared experience can lead you to take unnecessary risks in order to avoid them from happening to you. In other words, even if nothing happened to you, and you only heard about it from another, you could still be influenced to take unnecessary risks.

Watch your reactions carefully. See if *Confirmation Bias* is at play as I share some statistics and data that could help you form an unbiased decision. Are you reading the data and thinking some of these are right or some of these are wrong based on what you already believe? If so, that's *Confirmation Bias* at play. Do you find yourself getting defensive in some way? Is there a strongly held belief that you already have? I'd be interested to learn if you found yourself more convinced of your view if the data points the other way (the *Backfire Effect*).

> **Key Point:** Rather than determining if the data and ideas presented in this book fit your already existing beliefs, you could be looking to uncover a new path that supports your goals.

This obviously begs the question, what are your goals?

Real Estate Goals

Mostly, in my experience when people are selling, they're looking for some combination of:

1. The most money
2. In the least time
3. With the least hassle

When buying it's:

1. The best house
2. For the least money
3. In the least time
4. With the least hassle.

This is not unique to real estate. Most consumer transactions involve weighing factors like these. It's simply the singular expense, impact, and rarity of the act of buying or selling a home that makes this transaction especially worth examining.

Let's look at the data around selling a home first and look at it from the perspective of the typical goal of a seller as stated above.

The first fact I'd like to examine is the oft quoted National Association of Realtors' (NAR) study that shows homes that sold without an agent (FSBO) sell for about 13 percent less than homes sold by a Realtor. Anytime I see a study in which the results are so self-serving, it raises concerns of bias, intentional or unintentional. I don't trust the tobacco companies' studies on lung cancer or big oil's studies on climate change. Likewise, I can't take the claims of the NAR, or FSBO web sites for that matter, at face value.

Rather than rest on data from sources with an axe to grind, let's look at some simple data analysis right from the Multiple Listing Service (MLS). A quick note here: This is not in any way meant to be comprehensive of a national picture. The data was pulled from my local MLS – the NWMLS – and it includes Washington State only. This is not necessarily representative of a national picture. In fact, one of the big problems with the NAR study is that it attempts to make a point using national data when real estate is a hyperlocal phenomenon. I'm using this example to help you understand the information you could (and should) be seeking from your local real estate professionals.

Here's what I found: In 2017, homes worth more than $450,000 sold by owners, who listed in MLS, sold for 99% of asking price. Homes sold by real estate agents sold for, on average, 102% of asking price.

It's important to remember that most sellers used in the information above paid the agent who brought the buyer a commission of 2.5 to 3 percent. This means they only saved the listing agent commission, which was likely to be somewhere about the same. In other words, they likely saved 2.5 to 3 percent in fees, and then lost 3% in average sale price, netting no gain for going it alone.

First, you're going to need to determine what the actual numbers are in your area for homes like yours. It varies by price point, by city, and likely by neighborhood. Finding out the details of your situation matters.

Of course, it's up to you to decide. As you go through this book, you'll be able to see a little deeper, and with more clarity, into each step of the process of home selling and buying. Keep looking for where you might be used by one of these shortcuts, with the intention of slowing down and making rational decisions. By the end, you should have a clear idea what will make the most sense for you.

This data is fairly easy for an agent to access. It took me about an hour to gather it, so make any agent spewing that 13 percent national average number go find what's true in your case. If they aren't willing to do that, you might want to take that into consideration before you hire them.

What if you're a buyer? Does it make sense to represent yourself in an attempt to leverage a further discount from the seller?

It's commonly thought that since the buyers' agents' commissions are included in the price, and come out of the money the seller receives, the seller is paying that commission. I think that's disingenuous at best. Every month for the next 30 years or so, the buyer will be writing a check to cover the agreed price. It sure seems to me that the buyer is, in reality, paying both sides of the commission. From that perspective alone, it's worth reviewing to see if it makes sense, from a value standpoint, for a buyer to hire a representative in the transaction.

Unfortunately, there are no easily tracked statistics on the buy side that would show the dollar value of working with an agent or not. We can, however, lay out some of the soft costs and some of the likely places that having, or not having, representation might be worth it.

First, remember the seller has already priced the home with the understanding that they will be receiving the asking price less the agreed commission. With this in mind, approaching the seller with a proposal to provide a discount, since you're not using an agent, seems feasible, at least on the surface.

Of course, in practice, it's not quite so simple. Most states allow for something called "dual agency." This means the listing agent – the agent representing the seller – is also allowed to represent the buyer. Representing both sides allows that agent the opportunity to collect both sides of the commission. You approaching them without representation could look like a great chance to get paid double what they were planning on.

While the seller could technically demand their agent take less than the full value of both sides and give you some sort of discount, you'd have to wonder why they'd do that. Why wouldn't they demand their agent take less and pocket the savings themselves? After all, if the price they're asking is reasonable to begin with, why should they give you the difference? And who is going to negotiate that piece of the transaction? It's going to be you against their agent. In most cases, that means it will be you, who does this type of thing rarely, negotiating with someone who makes their living doing it and has a fiduciary interest in getting their client the most money.

Given this type of scenario, it's unclear that an unrepresented buyer can count on any discount in price. At best they might split the commission, let's say 1 to 1.5 percent, for a discount.

That's the money piece. To fully decide your best course of action, you'll need to add the other pieces of the equation, which include getting the best house, in the least time, with the least hassle. Assuming you can negotiate some sort of discount for going it on your own, are you clear and comfortable that, without representation, you're also getting the best house, in the least time and with less hassle?

Risking my obvious partisanship showing, I think the scenarios in which it makes sense for a buyer to commit to the unrepresented route are few and far between. Exceptions could include situations in which the buyer and seller are friends, family, or otherwise previously connected. In that case, where there's no agent involved on either side and there's healthy amount of trust, one lawyer and a good title company could be expected to generate sufficient savings to make sense.

Whether you're a buyer or seller, I recommend you read through each of the appropriate chapters to learn about the steps needed in the respective sides of the process. This will allow you to become responsible for any predictable shortcuts that might otherwise cloud or shape your judgments. From that unobscured vantage point, you'll be able to weigh the costs and benefits of having appropriate representation.

In the meantime, given the statistical likelihood of you doing so, I'm going to proceed as if you have chosen to hire a professional to represent you.

Chapter Five:

How and Who to Hire

"In looking for people to hire, you look for three qualities: integrity, intelligence, and energy. And if they don't have the first, the other two will kill you."

– Warren Buffett

Let's start the examination of the shortcuts most likely to mess with selecting an agent by looking at *Availability* and *Representativeness* – by far the biggest factors in how people choose a Realtor.

As I've mentioned, according to multiple sources (from the NAR to Zillow) 70 percent of consumers will hire the very first agent they talk to. This means they don't have a system to interview multiple agents and then compare answers to see who is the most likely to produce the desired outcome.

On the surface, this is crazy if not out-and-out scary. Your home is the single most expensive thing you'll ever buy or sell. It's a complex transaction, with a multitude of moving parts. It's something consumers take on only a few times in their lives. The time between transactions is usually long enough that the conditions in which they're acting are likely to be radically different. It's not the type of transaction that can be returned or exchanged. There's no practical recourse for either party once the sale is complete.

The impact of the transaction is going to be dealt with on a daily basis for many, many years.

That the average consumer's due diligence is comparable to the work one would do in deciding where to eat (ask friends, count stars on a website, go with the person with the most signs in the neighborhood or who sends the most postcards) should be more than a little disconcerting at best, and horror-film frightening at worst.

Even the people I've met who don't do this, who do interview multiple agents, generally ask the wrong questions. They ask questions from their own *Confirmation Bias*. That is, they have a gut feeling they already know what's important in an agent and find an agent who matches their preconceived ideas.

This is the heart of the matter for me. It's where this book and my own interest in psychological heuristics all started. I became fascinated by the clear lack of regard people use to select someone to represent them in this transaction. Rather than master taking advantage of this, which is what agents are taught to do, I decided to help people make better choices. And it's in selecting a Realtor, that out of everything we discuss in this book, where shortcuts are most easily seen driving the process.

As covered earlier, heuristics are our tried-and-true rules of thumb that help us survive. They have us make quick decisions when we're in complex situations with uncertain outcomes. They drive us toward decisions that, if not always accurate, will be less likely to get us killed. But what heuristics provide in speed, they lose in accuracy. In the home-buying/selling process, speed rarely provides the kind of dollars-and-cents value that accuracy does. On those occasions when speed does matter, it's more likely to be productive if the time was taken up front to make sure rational, thoughtful systems were established.

It'll be easiest to spot the shortcuts at play when you first realize that Realtors already know you're driven by these tendencies.

It's not just Realtors, of course. All marketers and advertisers recognize that people don't make rational buying decisions. Modern advertising has been refined to take maximum advantage of our predictable irrationality. Realtors, at the heart of it, are marketers... first of themselves, to get you to agree to allow them to represent you, and then they become, hopefully, a marketer of your home. To spot your own shortcuts, it might be easier to look at how Realtors operate and see if it plays into any of the likely biases we've talked about.

Consider newspaper and print advertising. I'm going to take a wild guess and say that nobody has looked to a newspaper to shop for a home in 25 years. Ever wonder why Realtors still place ads there? Ever wonder why in the world a Realtor would pay money to advertise homes that they've already sold? Think about it: They're paying money to put in front of you information that, from a functional standpoint, is irrelevant. That home is sold. But, it is highly functional for *them*. It puts their name in your mind as someone who has done something that one day you might need done for you.

They're paying to occupy "mind share." This is not a particularly radical concept in advertising. It's understood that you'll only be able to recall a certain number of brands when thinking of a product. For example, think of a cola, a vacuum cleaner, an athletic sneaker, and a luxury watch. Quick. Don't second guess. What are the first brands that come to mind? Most middle age Americans think of Coke, Hoover, Nike, and Rolex. Younger people might think Pepsi, Dyson, Adidas, and Apple (yes, the iWatch counts). The point is: there might two or three names that come to mind as an answer. Beyond that, you'd need to think, and the point of heuristics is they allow us to avoid thinking.

Realtors know this, so their efforts tend toward making sure you know they're around. That way, when the time comes for you to buy or sell, their name is the name in your mind. In advertising jargon, this is what is meant by "top of mind." Owning "mind share" is only effective because you're used by the *Availability Heuristic* when making purchasing decisions.

Realtors already know you're unlikely to interview anyone else. Realtors know they need only show up in your mind (i.e., be available to the mind with little to no effort) as someone who is *representative* enough of what a Realtor is "supposed" to look like.

Their job, then, becomes making certain you've seen enough of their signs in people's yards, enough pictures of houses sold in the newspapers or postcards, that they dress like you imagine a Realtor will dress, that they drive the kind of car a Realtor is supposed to drive, and to make sure they have enough stars next to their name online. They've learned the most important thing is to get to you first. If they've checked any of the other boxes, and are first to you, they will get hired 70 percent of the time.

They know you're never going to interview them in the way people interview someone for a job involving hundreds of thousands of dollars. The odds are high you're not going to ask them to show you their specific, personal performance, as it relates to your goals. They know you have no system to compare those results to the results of any other agent. They know it's a complex transaction, with an uncertain outcome, and you're going to lean on automatic thinking to get through this.

Even if you did, somehow, develop the view that there is a quantifiable difference between Realtors, you aren't prepared to know what to ask that separates them. Your predisposition to believing what you already know to be true is too strong to have you investigate further. In other words, the information stored and fed to you by the *Availability* and *Representative Heuristics* is too potent for your *Confirmation Bias* to ignore. Before I mentioned this here, it's unlikely you've ever seen anything beyond what these shortcuts allow you to see.

Think about it: Do you have the belief that all Realtors are pretty much the same? Why would you believe this? Do you believe that all doctors or lawyers or CPAs are pretty much the same? It's interesting, isn't it? I've spoken to a lot of potential clients, and whether they consciously believe this or not, their actions certainly indicate that this is how Realtors occur for them. That is, whether you admit this or not, if you're either hiring the first person you meet or are not quantifying the difference in the performance of the Realtors you're interviewing, then you'd have to admit that you either believe all Realtors are the same or believe there's no way to quantify the difference.

With what you now know about mental shortcuts, notice if you're defending your view. Is there some deeply held view that's threatened by my assertion? Are you clearer than ever that the person you hired the last time was the right choice because I'm suggesting you might have hired them irrationally? Thank the *Backfire Effect*. Nothing new is possible here and you might as well close this book and move on with your life.

Complicating the situation is that nobody actually wants a Realtor. What people want is to buy or sell their home. Unless examined, as we did at the start, Realtors will sort of come along with the package and be a process requirement for most. There's no real pull or desire to get into the weeds with someone when they're all the same anyway.

When it comes to selling a home, most people are totally in the dark about what it takes, but because of the fear of looking like a dope, people don't ask the right (or any) questions when hiring an agent. Realtors are specifically trained to appeal to this type of "non-thinking" and are shockingly unprepared to speak to their actual performance. They know if they can appeal to the *Availability* and *Representativeness heuristics, Confirmation Bias* will take over and get them the contract.

It Gets Worse

Ready for more bad news? There's hardly a professional service industry that has a lower bar to entry than real estate. The average barber has ten times more study hours under their belt than the average Realtor. That's right; the person at Sport Clips studied roughly 1,000 hours to give me my $20 haircut. Compare that to the person selling your half-million-dollar house who studied on average about 90 hours. In no state in the U.S. is the requirement for study more than 150 hours. The vast majority require 100 or fewer clock hours for licensing, which amounts to about two weeks of study.

Read that again if you must. The person you hired (or are going to hire) has studied for two weeks to get their license and let me tell you, I have never seen a less relevant, less useful, test in my life. To give you a sense of the depth of the stupidity, in Washington we need to learn the number rods in an acre, and while I may not be the sharpest crayon in the box, I'm pretty sure that's never going to be a pertinent calculation.

But wait, there's more! Last year, there were approximately two million licensed agents in the country who sold around 5.4 million homes. That's an average of 2.7 homes per agent. Even if you used Pareto's principle (that 20 percent of any group does 80 percent of the work, a reliable principle in my experience) and assumed that 20 percent of the available agents sold 80 percent of homes, you'd calculate that 400,000 agents sold 4.3 million homes or 11 homes per agent – that's not even one a month!

Not only are Realtors under (and poorly) trained compared to other professions, they get very little practice at their craft. If this doesn't at least open the possibility that having a structured way to separate agents based on their performance is a good idea, it has to be the ***Backfire Effect*** running the show over there.

Even Realtors reading this will acknowledge my point here. Every decent Realtor I've ever worked with has horror stories of being on the opposite side of the table with an agent who was so incompetent that there was no way their client could have interviewed them.

To be clear – I'm not saying Realtors are dishonest. I'm sure some are, but they're not the norm. Realtors are, like most everyone, taking what's given. If customers are only going to demand they be fast (*available*) and appear competent (*representative*), then that's what they're going to focus on.

This might be why a surprising number of Realtors seem to be playing some game other than "get my clients the best deal possible, in the least amount of time, with the least hassle." That we've already distinguished the reason they're not playing that game doesn't make it less surprising. There are too many agents who care for little more than getting the transaction closed so they can move on to the next one. After all, they don't need to get the best deal for their client if nobody is going to ask about it later. What they need to survive is another sign in another yard, another house to advertise as closed, and a pleasant review.

This all adds up to make for a bad situation for the consumer... you.

Realtors all seem to be helpful and pleasant but for the most part, their clients don't know how the game is played. At the risk of beating a dead parrot, let me say again: This is crazy scary!

For a transaction that's complex, life changing, and the most expensive thing you'll ever buy or sell, you're about to do it based solely on the recommendation of a coworker?

You're willing to trust that to your mother's best friend's husband?

You're going to put that deal in the hands of that lady you met at your school auction because you have a good feeling about her?

You're afraid it'll be awkward if you don't use your kid's soccer coach?

Or worse, you're going to apply the same rules you use to buy something on Amazon, or pick a restaurant on Yelp, and look for someone who has the best online reviews and/or the cheapest price?

This is why Realtors have such a bad reputation – because nobody's vetting them based on their actual performance!

It Gets Better

The good news is determining the likelihood that a particular Realtor is going to deliver above-average performance is simple. Now, it's not foolproof, but there are some surefire, telltale signs that separate an above-average Realtor from a mediocre one. In fact, with a simple interview format, anyone can feel confident that they've found the right person to represent them in this large, complex, and singularly impactful transaction.

As discussed in Chapter 3, mindset matters. You won't do this if you're thinking all Realtors are the same or there's no way to tell them apart. Try on the mindset I offered in Chapter 3. Become the CEO of a business that's selling (or buying) a commodity, and you're looking for the right COO to run that business.

This should be easy to create. After all, you're the one who has the home to sell (or the need to buy a home). You're the one bringing the money to the table and that makes you the boss. As the boss, you're now hiring someone to run your business.

Wouldn't it be smart if they had a track record of running businesses like yours successfully? Shouldn't they be both competent and trustworthy? And since you'll be spending a bit of time with them, shouldn't they be someone you enjoy spending time with? Shouldn't they be someone whose communication style works for you?

Quick quiz: What's the simplest way to find an employee with the above qualities? Yes! You'd interview them! In fact, you should plan on doing this in the same way you would interview anyone for any job that involves hundreds of thousands of your dollars... because this one does!

At the end of the day, I think people know they should do this. They don't, however, because they don't know what to ask, so rather than risk looking foolish, they just skip the interview.

I see this mistake cost people tens of thousands of dollars every day. In real estate, I realize that there's often an asymmetry of information. One side knows a lot more about the process than the other. The process of home buying or selling, for better or worse, is not transparent and it is complex. I recommend you spend time learning what you can on any number of useful websites.

But – and this is a big caveat – I don't care how much information you get from WebMD, if you believe that makes you a doctor, you're a fool. And if you pretend that Redfin or Zillow makes you a Realtor, you'll soon discover the truth behind the adage that a fool and their money are soon parted.

Now, let's look at the right questions to ask so you hire the right professional.

Chapter Six:

What to Look For

"Opportunity is missed by most people because it is dressed in overalls and looks like work."

– Thomas Edison

Now, with a better understanding of your dependency on mental shortcuts, the need to interview a Realtor before hiring them should be obvious. Still, you might not know what questions to ask. Let's clear that up right now.

What follows is a framework around which you can empower yourself with the right questions. Using this as a guide will not simply help you find a Realtor you can trust, you can trust your kid's soccer coach, I want you to find one you can trust *and* is most likely to produce the results you are looking for. Remember, all Realtors are not the same – and using this as a guide, you can tell the difference.

To start, think of all the normal things you'd consider when interviewing someone:

- Were they on time?
- Did they treat you with respect (or were they condescending)?
- Were they prepared?
- Were you left smarter for having spoken with them, or were you left confused?

- Did they handle the interaction like they were applying to run your business?
- Is this someone with whom you'd like to spend time?

Those are general rules of interviewing and have value in most scenarios. What follows are seven questions specific to real estate. These will allow you to see who's most likely to produce the results you want.

Are these the only questions? Of course not. In any sort of system that attempts to measure performance, they are, to a degree, arbitrary. That is, I've selected things to measure, at least partly, because they're easy to measure and simple to compare. Could you choose other things? Sure, you could, but be careful as I will also give some examples of questions that people think matter, but ultimately do not.

Question 1: How many transactions did you do last year?

Practice makes perfect (or at least improves performance). Given the statistics we covered earlier, you know most Realtors don't do a lot of business. Even using the 80/20 rule, many agents don't even transact one deal a month. Depending on where you live, that level of activity might not generate sufficient income to live on. This should beg the question: Do you want to hire someone who does real estate part time, has another job, or, worse, whose business is failing?

I recommend you find someone who does at least 15 to 20 transactions a year. Fewer than that and you should start to wonder, "Why? What's wrong with the way they do business that they can't, or aren't, doing at least a couple of deals every month?"

Someone doing less than a deal every month is doing this as a hobby, not a profession. They should be thanked for their time and you should move on. Let them learn on someone else.

I'd also be interested in how many transactions they've done so far this year. Why? Because if they're not on track to match last year's performance, you might want to know why. This would also be a good time to ask how long they've been in the business. For example, someone in the business for 10 years who's doing 20 transactions per year might not be hustling the same way someone just starting out who's done 14 their first year.

The answers to these questions will not only give you insight into their business but the market as a whole. If the market is strong and their business isn't growing, I'd be concerned they might have something else going on in their life that's taking precedence over their business. On the other hand, if the market is weak and their business is growing, I'd be more confident that they're doing something right.

Note: This is a qualifying question. That is, if they aren't doing 15 to 20 per year, then you might want to pass on them. It's not saying the guy who does 100 is better than the lady doing 30. It sets a floor. It isn't about more always being better.

Question 2: How do you get most of your business?

While this might seem like an odd question, it can tell you a lot about the person you're considering hiring.

A Realtor getting the majority of their business through referrals and repeat business runs one kind of business. A Realtor who gets most of their business through internet leads runs a different kind of business.

An agent who gets at least 50 percent of their business from referrals and repeat business could be expected to have business systems that make themselves useful after the sale. This underscores their understanding that a successful real estate business is based on long-term relationships.

Someone whose business model relies on generating a steady flow of "cold" leads is likely to have less time and energy to focus on taking care of clients after the sale. They're more likely to be running a transaction-based business than they are a relationship-based business.

This is not conclusive information – don't eliminate someone for one answer or the other. Yet it's helpful in being able to determine who's going to be more likely to handle some of the items that show up your list of "hassles" you're asking a Realtor to handle.

Question 3: Do you have a team or are you solo?

Hiring a Realtor who's on a team or who runs a team is preferable. Why? Because there is no way for an agent to be all things to all their customers, unless they only have one customer.

The number one complaint I hear from people about their last agent was that they didn't communicate enough or that they somehow felt their agent didn't have time for them.

You already know I'm recommending you hire someone who does a lot of business. Unless they have a team working with them to address the details that arise throughout the process, you run the risk they won't have time for you.

Ask them who their team members are. This varies widely, and there's no one right answer. You want to know they have both the office staff to handle the paperwork and logistics of the transaction, as well as other trained agents who can communicate and work with you should your agent not be available.

Find out if the person you're interviewing will be working with you personally at every step, or do they have specialists to handle various aspects of the transaction. There are advantages and disadvantages either way, but the important thing is you understand this before you begin the process and you're comfortable with how they do it.

Ask if they have vacations planned during your anticipated transaction timeline. I've started and closed deals for clients while I was on vacation, so again, there's no "right" answer, but as the

CEO doing the hiring, you need to know. Find out if they have hours or days during which they don't work. Some real estate agents don't work after 6:00 p.m. or on Sundays. Is that okay with you? Some people like their employees to be available nights and weekends and some people are less demanding. It's up to you to decide what you're looking for in an employee.

Question 4: What is your commission?

Ah, the question about money. It is not, however, the money question. That's the next one.

This question provides your chance to check on their negotiation skills. Overall in the U.S., the typical commission is usually somewhere around six percent. This is split between two agents: three percent for the buyer's agent and three percent for the listing agent. You can do an internet search and find the average for your market.

A quick word or two here about discount brokerages seems appropriate. Discount brokers offer, surprise, a discount. While I'd find it very difficult to believe that you like a bargain more than I do, there are certain things for which I do not search for bargains. I don't want a discount defense attorney (I've never needed one; I'm just sayin'). If someone in my family, heaven forbid, needed a medical specialist, I also would likely not shop based on price.

Before you jump at the next discount broker think about why businesses offer discounts in the first place. Discounts anywhere in business always mean one of two things:

1. *They plan to make it up on volume*. Think Costco and Amazon. They have lower overhead and/or they sell in bulk. Sometimes a discount will be offered if the company is venture funded and isn't required to turn a profit yet. Sometimes the product is a "loss leader" and the company will make their money on another offering. At the end

of the day, they're using their lower price to attract a larger volume of customers. The smaller profit margin is compensated by a larger number of sales now, or in the future.

2. ***The product, offering, or service is of lower value and the market will not pay full price for it.*** In other words, they'd love to get full price for what they're selling, but the market won't pay it. Overstocks, cheap imports, and knock offs all fall into this category.

That's it. It always comes down to one of those two scenarios. This is not a real estate thing. This is a business thing. Let's examine each one, so you can best determine why you're being offered a discount.

Are they offering a discount as some sort of loss leader, or come on, and they'll add fees for different services later? Are they a startup trying to attract market share? Many discount brokerages, thinking they're upending an archaic industry, start out by offering huge discounts in effort to gain customers, and then over time, those discounts disappear. If you've followed the history of Redfin, this is precisely what has happened. Does that mean you shouldn't grab a discount when it's offered? Of course not. But be aware that the discount they're offering may not be because they found some better way to do things. It could be that they're investor funded and aren't constrained by operating at a profit yet. Make sure the end results, and not just the price of entry, are better for you.

Consider it at the level of the individual agent who's talking to you right now, the actual person you're interviewing. You must at least consider that if this person could charge a full commission (that is, if people would pay them the full market rate), that's what they'd be asking you for. The fact that they're asking for less would at least give me pause that, maybe, there's some quality issues involved. What corners are they cutting? Why aren't they asking for the going rate? Are they new and don't feel comfortable asking for full price? I recommend you find out. I'm not convinced any of those scenarios put you in the best position for what is the most expensive transaction of your life.

This is also true if they start out as a full-price agent, but you're able to negotiate them down on commission. You need to keep in mind that a big piece, perhaps the largest piece, the value a good Realtor provides is their ability to negotiate the best possible price for you. This is quantifiable (as you'll see later), and asking this question will allow you to see how well they negotiate.

> **Key Point:** How they negotiate with you is a direct indicator of how they will negotiate for you. If they cannot negotiate well with you for their fee, what are the odds they will negotiate well to defend your equity?

Think about it: If you're an average home seller, you don't sell very many homes, especially when compared to a professional Realtor. So here you are, someone with very little background in real estate negotiations, and you have just moved your Realtor down ½ percent on their commission. You probably feel pretty good about that. What you're overlooking is that the Realtor you're working with just got out negotiated by you, someone with little experience, while trying to defend their own money! How quickly are they going to fold when faced with a professional Realtor at the very time you're counting on them to defend your money? Pennywise and pound foolish?

By the way, this is why every full-service Realtor I know loves negotiating against a discount broker. They tend to be younger and less experienced... and they have already told the world they can't even negotiate their own price because, again, if they could get full price for their services, wouldn't they?

It's almost always the discount agent's plan to work on volume, which means they may not be focused on building a long-term relationship; they might just as soon spend a few more of your dollars, get the deal done, and move on.

Question 5: What is your list-to-sales price ratio, and how does that compare to the local market?

Now, this is the real money question. The answer will tell you two things:

First, do they know, and can they communicate, the current market conditions as they pertain to you? Are they speaking in a way that actually communicates to you? How they explain this is critical as there are many details throughout the transaction, and this question can help you determine if they're competent at communicating.

Do they make sure you understand what they're saying or are they rushed, unsure, and confused? Do they make you feel smart for asking, and are you smarter (more informed) for having asked?

Second and more importantly, you'll learn about their actual performance. If you're in buying mode, they should be able to show you that they've negotiated prices below market average. If you're selling, they should be able to show you they get more than market average. *If their performance isn't better than average, you'll need some other really good reason to hire them.*

This is so basic I'm shocked people don't ask this question! How could you ever trust that you are getting the best possible deal without seeing both: what is actually happening in the market, and how a particular agent performs in that market? Remember: This is your business. You're hiring someone to run your business. Your business is worth hundreds of thousands of your dollars. Please make sure you get someone who is competent and has a track record in successfully handling businesses like yours.

More than anything else they say during your interview, these numbers are their "track record." It's what you can use to gauge how effectively they do their job.

> **Key Point:** While past performance doesn't guarantee future performance and every home sale presents a unique situation, if you're expecting a Realtor whose past performance is below average to suddenly get you more money for your home than average, you need to explain to me how that's going to work.

It's possible, and maybe even likely, that the Realtor you're interviewing might not know this information off hand. From one perspective, this is forgivable as we've already established they're almost never asked for it, so why would they have it? At the same time, you gotta think, "Why should someone have to ask them for their performance before they'd bother to go find out what it is? What have they been using to measure their performance?"

Most real estate agents know how many transactions they've done and the dollar volume of those transactions. That's nice... for them! That's how they did for themselves, not how well they did for their clients. That they know one number (transactional dollar volume) and not the other (the amount they got their clients over or under average) says a lot about where they focus their attention – on their own business rather their clients'.

One possible way to get this information is to ask them to send you their last 12 months of sales right from the MLS. It's easy for them to get and will have all the information you want. It should have the listing date, listing price, sale date, and sale price. Now you can compare days on market and list-to-sales price for each potential agent. This is a super easy way to create a level playing field for everyone you are interviewing.

Be clear that every market has different conditions and different agents employ different marketing strategies. Some will price homes under market value to drive multiple offers and get more money. This strategy in particular might skew the results of this question in their favor.

In other words, just because Agent Bob sells homes at five percent over list price and Agent Sarah sells three percent below list price, you still don't necessarily know the whole story. Agent Sarah could be setting the bar high and, at the end of the day, still be putting more money in the seller's pocket even though it's less than asking.

You'll need to ask each agent to explain their predominant strategy, so you can get a better idea of how they've actually performed. *However, it's a big mistake to pretend that because agents can, and do, employ different strategies, there's no way of comparing them.* Their performance can, and must, be measured.

Question 6: Can I have three or four references to call, please?

Okay, the trick here is that you need to call people. Call their references! Seriously, pick up the phone and call them. You're conducting interviews for a job; calling references is what you do. And yes, I understand that they're only going to give you references of people who will speak well of them. That's no different than any other applicant to any other job. People still call job references before hiring, and you should, too.

When you call, ask how much over (for a sale) or under (for a buy) the deal was and how many days it was on market. Ask if anything didn't work or didn't go well. Ask if there's anything they regret with their transaction. Where did the agent fail to deliver? Online reviews will never tell this story. This is the most expensive, complicated transaction of your life and it requires special measures.

Online reviews are fine but actually speaking to someone who worked with the agent you're considering is always better. It's one thing to ask a client to write an online review; it's another to ask if they're willing to take calls from other prospective clients.

If the Realtor you're interviewing came to you via a trusted source, maybe you don't need to call anyone else. That's your choice. But if this is a Realtor who you found on the internet or from some other source, you'd do well to speak to people who have used them before.

Question 7: At what price would you list my home and what do you think it will sell for?

Here's another chance to talk strategy. Probably the most important factor here is to ask them to show you the evidence that supports their price. Make them show you the comparable properties (comps).

> **Key Point:** Never choose an agent simply because they say they'll sell your home for the highest price – unless, of course, they're buying it themselves.

This is a critical question. Anyone can tell you they can sell it for any amount. Less scrupulous agents could attempt to "*buy your listing*." This is when an agent tells the seller they can sell it for the amount they think the seller wants to hear, even if there's no evidence to support that price. Why would they do that? Because:

1. They get to put a sign in your yard, and we already talked about the value that creates for the agent (*Availability Heuristic*). Whether your home sells or not, people will see the sign and give up a little mind share each time.
2. They will get the "sign calls." People will see the sign (or the listing online) and call for information. Given your home is overpriced, they won't be interested in buying your home, but the agent is now the

first one in front of the caller, and they can work to become their agent for a different, more reasonably priced house.

By telling you what you want to hear rather than the truth, the agent can turn your house into more business for them regardless whether they sell your home or not.

This is why it's so important to ensure the evidence they present regarding the price of your home makes sense to you. Selling your house is your business; make sure you can own their recommendations. The buck stops with you. The most appropriate way to look at the value of your home is to look at it from the perspective of a buyer: Based on what's available in the market right now, how much would you pay for your home?

The section of this book dedicated to selling your home will get deep into pricing strategy and will help make more sense of this. Don't interview an agent without reading it.

If you're a buyer, this question isn't relevant. Instead, you can ask, "Given what I'm looking for (this includes location and size of home), how long should it take you to find something that will work for me?" If you can afford to wait before you buy, I recommend you ask, "What's the best time of year for me to be shopping in my area?" They should be able to provide you with historical trends that show the seasonality of your market and when you're more likely to find the best deals.

In all cases, you're looking for someone who's going to be straight with you and who demonstrates having your best interests at heart. Are they interested in you buying or selling now, even though the seasonal trends would indicate waiting is better? Do they even know the seasonal tendencies and how they impact buyers vs. sellers? They need to know because you need to know, and you need to know because, after all, it's your business!

Summarizing the Surveys

Whether you're buying or selling, the way the Realtor answers these questions is almost as important as the actual answers. While these questions and their answers will help you determine which real estate agent is right for you, the best rule of thumb is to continue to ask questions until you're comfortable with the situation and the person.

Like I said before – almost nobody does this kind of interview. Don't be surprised if the Realtor you talk to has never seen anything like this. Be aware that they might not be prepared with all this information at their fingertips as nobody ever asks them for it. While someone who does have this information ready and available might be a better choice, it's probably worth giving an agent who doesn't have it readily available a day or two to pull it together.

Regardless, in no case should you be made to feel stupid or overly protective or annoying or like a pest for asking these questions. Anybody who feels that they don't have the time to answer these questions is unlikely to understand what it means to have a fiduciary responsibility to you. They should be dismissed from consideration as quickly as possible.

Remember, you're looking to hire a business partner. If they don't express a partnership interest with you, why would you hire them?

You can start the interview process by gathering the names of possible agents – get these from friends, ask for them on Facebook, find popular agents on Zillow, etc. Once you get the list together, to save time, and any socially awkward situations, email them the seven questions while explaining what you're doing.

The email could look something like this:

Dear <agent's name>,

I'm considering selling my home at <location>and you came recommended to me by <referral's name>. {Alternatively, you could say: "I found you online and your reviews are impressive."}

I'm in the process of interviewing real estate agents and would love to see your answers to the questions below.

1. *How many transactions did you do last year and how many so far this year?*
2. *What percentage of your business is referral or repeat business?*
3. *Do you have a team or are you a solo agent?*
4. *What is your commission?*
5. *What is your list-to-sales price ratio and how does that compare to the local market?*
6. *Can you send me three or four references for me to call?*
7. *My address is <street address>. How much do think you would sell my home for?*

Thanks for taking the time to answer these questions. I'll compile all the responses I receive and be in touch should I wish to do an in-person interview.

To save you time, you can download an editable version of this pre-interview email at www.rationalrealestate.pro/interview.

This makes it simple and non-confrontational for you to pre-screen potential Realtors. After you've determined who has the track record that's likely to produce your goals, you can then take the time to meet them face to face. Energy, synergy, gut feelings are important, too. You'll be spending a lot of time with this person; make sure they're simpatico with your style.

Questions You Don't Need to Ask

There are at least two questions many people will ask that are of no help in separating a good agent from a mediocre one, so let me clear those up, too.

First, people have it in their heads that getting an agent who sells a lot of homes in a particular neighborhood is important. And second, people somehow think judging a Realtor's marketing plan is something they're qualified to do.

Let's start with the dispelling "Myth of the Neighborhood Agent." I'm pretty certain I know how this got started, and if for some reason, you subscribe to the notion that an agent with a history in a particular neighborhood is important, I'm sorry to say, you've been duped. While having knowledge of specific areas might be of value when shopping for a home ("might" being the key word there), there is almost no case to be made for the advantage "knowing" a neighborhood makes to the agent listing and selling a home.

Tell me something: When you bought the home you're in now, did you even talk to the listing agent? Did you, as a buyer, even think of what the listing agent knew or didn't know about the neighborhood? What difference did it make to you, as a buyer, if the agent the seller hired had sold any houses in the neighborhood in the past?

You do know that your agent is literally never going to speak to, nor are they likely to meet, the buyer. The person you hire is not there to talk to buyers. The only knowledge they need about your neighborhood is the past sales history, which is all available in public records.

Maybe if you live in a condo with an odd set of restrictions would a history of sales in the building help. Other than that, how many homes they've sold in the area matters very little compared to the dollar amount over or under average they sell.

Far more important is to see the prices of the homes they've sold. Selling a million-dollar home is very different than selling a $300,000 rambler. But the area in which the house sits matters not at all.

When you look at this more closely, you'll see the reason many people think the "neighborhood agent" matters is a function of *Availability* and *Representativeness* and nothing more. If you think this superstition makes a material difference, I promise it's more a function of heuristics than actual benefit provided to the seller. People think neighborhood agents matter because they're more familiar with them; that is, they are more *available* to the mind.

By the way, Realtors love this. It's way easier for an agent to pick a neighborhood, saturate it with marketing, nurture relationships in one geographic area and dominate that area than it is to schlep all across the city. They know it's easier to convince people to work with them when they are familiar with their name, so they promote themselves as the neighborhood expert.

Realtors even have a name for this. They call a specific geographic region they're out to dominate "a farm" and call the marketing they do "farming." If you follow that logic to its natural conclusion, it'll be pretty clear that given they're farming your neighborhood, that makes you the crop.

Bottom line? If you think an agent is better suited to sell your home just because they've sold other homes on your block, then congratulations – you're ripe and ready for harvesting.

The second thing people attempt to use to select the better agent is the difference between agents' marketing plans. Don't get me wrong; as you'll see in Chapter 19, I think marketing is critical to getting the most money in the least time. I just can't imagine how you'd be able to judge one marketing plan from another without *Representativeness* and *Confirmation Bias* being the source of the conclusion.

What are you looking for in a marketing plan that looking at their past sales won't tell you? Suppose Agent Sally touts the way her kiosk at the mall really brings the buyers in, and Agent Bob doesn't have a mall kiosk but tells you how great Facebook is at attracting the right people. Who do you choose? How would you even begin to know? Without looking at who sold homes for more money in less time, you have nothing but your already existing notions of what works. That's what **Representativeness** and **Confirmation Bias** looks like in action.

With both these questions, the proof of the pudding is in the tasting. Don't worry about their insider knowledge or their marketing plans. It either shows up in the last 12 months of sales or it doesn't. If they sell homes for less than average, you need to assume what they're doing, or how they're doing it, doesn't work. If they sell homes for more than average, then it works. Period.

Summary

Will all this make your decision completely rational? No, but it will put you on the right track to having some rational way to choose your representation.

I've intended to provide a way to clear out the shortcuts from making the choice for you. The rest of this book shines a light on what might otherwise be unseen during each phase of the transaction.

Last Thought: If you still want to hand your business over to your cousin's best friend, or the lady you met at the school auction, or your kid's soccer coach because it would be socially awkward to choose someone else, you can still do so. Social capital is real and it has value. The methodology above is simply a way to add a dollar amount to that capital, so you have more control over your choice.

Ready to take a peek into the black box of real estate? Let's do it.

Section 2:

Buying

Chapter Seven:

The "Pre's"

"Give me six hours to chop down a tree and I will spend the first four sharpening the axe."

– Abraham Lincoln

In these next chapters, we'll explore the distinct steps that are most common to the buying process. I'll also give you an opportunity to look for the shortcuts that, if left undistinguished or ignored, could cost you time, money, and maybe even the home of your dreams.

Keep in mind the context you invented: You're the CEO of a company and, in this case, you're out to buy a commodity in a crowded marketplace. With this as a backdrop, the material in this chapter becomes the due diligence phase.

Finding and buying a home is a journey, and it can be a long one, so doing your due diligence will help your stress level, your sanity, and maybe even allow you to enjoy the ride. In this case, being prepared not only includes doing the traditional work of getting pre-approved for a loan and learning your market, but also being on the lookout for where you might be led astray by mental shortcuts and heuristics. In a world where time is money, being prepared can often save you both.

Look, I hate preparing for anything. I hate packing; I hate studying; I hate anything that isn't doing the thing itself. But taking the time to prepare, and to understand all the steps, will allow you to secure the best possible deal for yourself with the least amount of frustration.

Note, I said "least frustration" as you shouldn't expect it to be eliminated completely. Forget about the fact this is one of the most expensive, impactful, and complicated transactions you're ever going to have; on top of all that, it involves moving! That means it involves packing and sorting through all your stuff. Everything you own needs to be physically handled, sorted, packed (or sold or tossed), and moved... and then unpacked, handled, and placed somewhere useful. This alone makes the whole transaction stressful beyond what most are prepared for. I've never met anyone who loved this part – the moving part. The act of moving, with or without the added stress of purchasing a property, is, for almost everyone, right up there with root canals and tax audits in terms of fun. So, no, it'll never be 100 percent stress-free.

I'm not out to be some Gloomy Gus about this, but it sets up an impossible-to-fulfill expectation to think this will be all fun and games. I find when people are realistic about their expectations things are far less stressful.

Now that that's settled, and you're clear there will be some frustration along the way, here's what you need to know to minimize both the frustration and your stress level.

Getting Pre-Qualified and Pre-Approved

The first step to take, whether you want to or not, is to get your money right and get your finances in order. It's pretty obvious nobody wakes up and says, "Oh, yeah baby, I'd love to take out a loan today!" Nobody wants a loan. People want a home. But the reality is that if you want to buy a house, you're most likely going to need a loan. (Of course there are cash buyers who don't need a loan, but that's an exception, not the rule.)

As the CEO of a new company out to make a major purchase, you'll need a very clear understanding of how much money you have available to spend. If you start visiting open houses, or perusing the internet for available properties, without first knowing your own financial picture, you're both wasting your time and setting yourself up for disappointment. Imagine finding your dream house in the perfect neighborhood with the exact layout, charm, and character you want, only to discover later that you can't afford it. Bummer!

If you do fall in love with a home you can't afford, besides disappointment, you'll also be subjected to *Anchoring* as you move through the process. That is, once you do establish your price range, you'll have already become *anchored* to a home that's too expensive. Now, every other property you find will pale in comparison to that perfect, albeit unaffordable, house on which you had your heart set. Don't be a victim of this shortcut. Establish your price range before you shop.

Now is the time to find a good lender so let's look at the typical shortcuts that can leave you shortchanged.

What makes a lender a "good lender"? If you shop on price, you might think it's rates, which, while important, are rarely the factor that separates a good lender from a not-so-good one. Rates vary based on the loan program you choose and can change hourly. Even within any one lending institution, the rate you wind up with can differ from the rates advertised. Many don't realize lender fees are negotiable so what a loan winds up costing you can be adjusted.

Like anything, price matters. But those shopping based on price (in this case, rates) will often find themselves with substandard service. Warren Buffet said "Price is what you pay. Value is what you get." Listen to Warren on this one. Shop for a lender based on value. With just a bit of effort, it's likely you can find someone who is both great to work with and has great rates.

Remember – the purchase of a home is not a simple transaction. It's expensive, it's fraught with emotions, there are many moving parts, and the implications of it last for many, many years. In my view, this isn't a place go cheap and cut corners.

Just as I recommend you interview multiple agents, I recommend you interview multiple lenders. CEOs select their investors with care and are picky about where they get their funding. Using unknown, faceless internet lenders or the bank you happen to use just because they come to mind easily (the *Availability Heuristic* at play) is crazy.

Look for a lender that:
- Only sells home loans
- Has a demonstrable track record of closing on time
- Operates as a consultant to develop a personalized strategy for obtaining the best loan product
- Has a good, personal relationship with the underwriting department
- Is accessible before, during, and after the transaction to help with any questions or problems

This is why I recommend you stay away from big banks, internet-based loan companies, most credit unions, and even smaller banks (not all, but most). Rarely do they meet the criteria above, with big banks being the worst. Really. I've personally never had a deal close on time when the buyer insisted on using one. Never. And while that's admittedly not the largest data set, I've yet to hear from an agent who prefers using a big bank. In almost every case where a big bank was used, my clients wish they had taken my advice and used a small, local mortgage lender of some kind.

In almost every case in which a client came to me wanting to use their big bank for the loan, the reason they gave was that it was simplest solution for them and not that they had vetted many alternatives. They hadn't determined through a screening process of any kind that their bank was the best choice, the criterion they used was they already bank there. Pure *Availability* and *Representativeness* in action. There was no thought given to the moving parts or how the bank performs, or might fail to perform, when the buyer needs them most. These buyers used their bank because that bank was at the top of their mind when they thought of getting a loan. Hello!? The word bank is synonymous with a place to get loans – you can't get more *representative* than that. Even though in a competitive market your ability to close on time could make or break the deal, few consider this aspect when choosing where to get their money. It's a pretty impactful shortcut.

As with Realtors, banks know that they can get your business by focusing on getting to you first. The reality of your susceptibility to the *Availability Heuristic* trains the banks the same as it trains Realtors. They both know their actual performance can take a back seat to speed. They don't need to be good to get your business. They just need to get to you first. The masses are driven by *Availability* and *Representativeness* and your bank knows this. Every time you walk in (or log in) to your bank, you see that person smiling at the desk, the signs and ads for what great rates they have, and it's pretty much over. They own your mind share. They don't need to worry that their loan underwriters are underpaid, work 2,000 miles away, and can't be reached easily when needed. Nobody is going to tell you that the smiling person in your branch, your loan officer, is almost as disconnected from the process as you are and won't be able to help when something goes south.

But of course, they don't care about that because they don't need to care. They aren't getting customers based on the strength of their service or the performance they deliver. They're getting the customers because they're masterful at creating and keeping mind share.

If you start the home-buying process with your Realtor, they will undoubtedly have a preferred lender or two to whom they'll be glad to refer you. If you don't have a lender you love, use theirs. Interview them to make certain you're simpatico and their rates and service are acceptable. The Realtor gets nothing from referring them to you. There are strict, well-enforced laws preventing any kind of kick back in that relationship. Your Realtor's only motivation is to have you use a lender who has proven track record of delivering products and services that get the job done.

Think about it: If the lender your real estate agent refers you to doesn't get the job done, who are you going to think poorly of and blame? And since we already know that you hired a Realtor who relies on your referrals and repeat business, they're likely to be super careful about the lender referrals they provide. It's a fair expectation that anyone they recommend will deliver. If you've already been pre-approved (as you should have been before shopping) and your Realtor recommends a different lender (because you've made a poor choice by picking a big bank, internet-based lender, etc.), I suggest you repeat the pre-approval process with the recommended lender.

It's also important to keep in mind the fact that the Realtor and lender have worked together in the past is not inconsequential. As you'll see in later chapters, moving a deal from contract to close is not simple. Selecting a team that already works well together, as a Realtor and lender will need to do, is a smart move.

I could write for days about this but will spare you. Suffice it to say, if you insist on going with your big bank, I wish you good luck and Godspeed. Just don't say I didn't warn you!

Popping the Question

As part of your preparation, the question you're out to have answered is simple: "How much house can I afford?"

To answer this, the lender will have to collect information from you. It could be during an initial phone call, a web-based survey or an in-person meeting. With some basic information and based on a series of formulas, they'll give you a ballpark sense of how much you can afford to spend on a house. This happens before they collect any documentation and is known as pre-qualification.

Pre-qualification is the least you need if you're just starting to think about a home purchase. It will help you keep your "browsing" in realistic neighborhoods with more realistic property sizes and amenities.

However, and this is a pretty big however, I recommend you take the next step – even if you're "just shopping" – and get pre-approved. In a seller's market, it's required. Pre-qualification is for your benefit only. You won't be able to place a viable offer on a property in any sort of competitive market if you're only pre-qualified.

Side Note: If you're shopping in a market that's even slightly competitive, I can't imagine any good Realtor who'd be willing to take you to see houses more than once, if you're only pre-qualified and not pre-approved. In most cases if you find an agent willing to drive you around before you've done the work to get pre-approved, I'd think they have too much time on their hands and might not be very good at what they do. Why else would they spend that kind of time on someone who wasn't serious yet?

Even if you think you're a year out from making a purchase, it still makes sense to get pre-approved for a loan. Here's why: In the pre-approval process, your lender is going to collect a wide range of documentation including pay stubs, bank statements, W-2s, etc. They're going to review your finances, and, if the lender is good and has your best interests at heart, they will do so with a fine-toothed comb.

All this so you wind up with a pre-approval for a loan. In essence, you want the lender to say, "Yes, we have seen all we need to see from this person and we're ready to write them a loan; the only thing we need is the address."

The process will bring up anything and everything that's between you and getting a loan in a way that pre-qualifying conversations won't. Suppose you're a year or more out and discover a blip on your credit report, a problem with the documentation of income, or if you'd qualify for a better loan with a little more down payment. Given you started early, you now have time to address those issues. Get pre-approved as early in the process as possible – it will save both time and money down the road.

I've encountered my share of clients who resist doing this early in the process. It's a particular form of **Confirmation Bias** expressed in the belief that they already know they'll be pre-approved, so why bother? I've encountered an equal number of people who, thanks to the same bias, won't go through the process because they already know they'll never be approved, so why bother?

The safer, less risky question is, "Why not bother?" The downside of waiting is, if there's something discovered in your finances with which the lender will have a problem, you won't have time to correct it. The downside of getting pre-approved early? Call me when you find one.

Once you're pre-approved, you'll know exactly how much house you can afford to buy, and you'll be ready to take the next step.

Pre-Shopping Consultation

You've talked to a lender, you have your pre-approval, and you're ready to go. That means you're ready for the second step (the fun part!) – meeting with a Realtor and starting to match your wants with your means.

It's possible the amount for which you're pre-approved may be more than you're comfortable with when it comes to monthly mortgage payments. You don't have to spend every dollar for which you're pre-approved. In fact, I recommend you always spend under your max. While, it's not a great way to market my business as a Realtor, it's a matter of integrity to let you know all houses are money pits. There's a never-ending list of possible ways to upgrade, improve, remodel, etc. Houses have a fascinating way to find a use for any extra money. With this knowledge, it's important that you're comfortable with the monthly payment and are honest about that with your Realtor.

When you do meet with your Realtor, share what you have in mind regarding the type of house you want and need:
- Number of bedrooms
- Number of bathrooms
- Location
- Possible school district or zone
- Yard space
- Garage
- Construction style

Add to this list whatever matters to you.

At this point, and with the information you've provided regarding price and what you want in a house, your Realtor should sit down with you and show you where houses that match your budget and your wants/needs are located.

Think about this process as having three facets: what you want to pay, what you want the house to look like, and where you want to house to be. It helps to go into this phase understanding you might only be able to get two out of three of these. It's rare enough to get everything you want in any area of life and the home-buying process is no different. If you hang on to some illusion that you must get every single thing on your list, you're setting yourself up for an upset. You could get lucky and get everything you want, but it's more likely that some compromise will be in order.

Normally price is not one with a lot of wiggle room so that leaves either size/amenities or location on which to be flexible. This is the step of the process in which you'll need to get clear about the difference between a "want" and a "need" with the "two out of three rule," being a small way to help keep your sanity.

This pre-shopping phase is the time to learn (and accept) where and how you might have to compromise on price, location, or amenities. This is the time to measure how realistic or unrealistic your expectations may be. If it's the latter, now is the time to make those mental adjustments. Can you afford to live where you want and in the type of house you want? This is the time to answer that question.

Remember: Real estate is cyclical. There will be times when any given market area could be a buyer's market (meaning lots of houses to choose from, prices staying steady or heading lower) or a seller's market (few houses for sale, prices head up). If you happen to be shopping in a buyer's market, you're less likely to need to compromise, and if you're in a seller's market, you'll likely need to move off your point to get the home you want.

Watch for the *Anchoring Heuristic* at play here as well. Perhaps you remember what houses cost the last time you bought a home, so there's some expectation of what you should pay now. Or perhaps you have an *anchor* in the form of the type and size of the home you grew up in, making shopping for your current home disappointing, frustrating, and/or upsetting.

I've seen this come up for people after they lost out on a house they loved. Now every other house is compared to that one — it became an *anchor* of sorts. Not only does every other house not quite measure up, but now every new house needs to represent the same price-to-size ratio as the one they lost.

The single biggest contributor to upsets and frustrations from *Anchoring* is brought to you courtesy of Zillow. Unless you've started your home search because you've been living in a cave, you know what Zillow is. It's also likely you've seen their algorithm-driven home valuation called the Zestimate. It looks very slick on their very slick website. But don't let looks fool you. The Zestimate is trash. It's dangerous, damaging, trash. By Zillow's own accounting, the Zestimate has a median margin of error of five percent. This means half their guesses are more than five percent off and half are less. Of course, you don't know which half your home falls in, so it's as practical as throwing darts at a board.

By way of illustrating the absurdity of thinking the Zestimate is somehow connected to reality, when Spencer Raskoff, the CEO of Zillow, listed his home for sale, the Zestimate turned out to be 40 percent higher than the sale price he received. If Zillow is off by 40 percent of their CEO's home, how accurate do you think it's going to be for you?

As we know by now, the accuracy and validity of an *anchor* has nothing to do with its impact. Virtually every client I talk with understands, intellectually at least, that the Zestimate is functionally useless when shopping. Yet, it's out there for everyone to see and is, without a doubt, creating an *anchor*.

I'll discuss this further when it comes to selling your home, but it applies to buyers as well. Buyers consider it when looking at the amount they are willing to offer on a home they're interested in. It's a shortcut-driven mistake, but people do it.

I don't have any illusions about you avoiding the Redfin or Zillow sites and their algorithmically generated values. That's unlikely to happen. But you can countermand the impact by asking your Realtor to do a custom valuation for any home you're interested in. Leave the Zestimates to less savvy buyers who don't know how their own mental shortcuts are affecting them. You're smarter than that now!

Un-Reality TV

Additionally, you should use the pre-shopping consultation to get answers to any questions you may have about buying a foreclosure, a short sale, or a fixer-upper. I'm afraid the slew of HGTV "reality" TV shows about fixing/flipping/remodeling houses that go from disaster to the cover of *Architectural Digest* in 30 minutes have romanticized a fantasy. Watching these shows, one could have what is **representative** of a good value shift toward fixer uppers. Watch enough and what's **available** to your mind could be how easy/simple/frequent remodeling is. While this is fine if you have the accompanying skill set to do the work, most people do not. As I've said, every home is a money pit. Starting in a hole is a much greater challenge than as seen on TV.

These shows could be said to create an **anchor** of sorts – "If they can do it, so can I." I always think they should come with one of those, "Don't try this at home" disclaimers. Ask your agent, given your needs, is this something you're ready for? Many businesses fail because the CEO is over confident in their abilities, so they take on more than they can handle. Don't make that mistake.

Getting all your questions answered helps you and your Realtor understand your expectations and the market. Your own searching can now be more valuable and they can begin to send you various listings they find that will be suitable for you to consider.

Then, and only then, are you ready to get in the car and visit properties.

Avoid Being Shortchanged: Shortcuts to Watch For

- *Availability Heuristic*: Using your bank as your lender because they come to mind when you think of getting a loan is crazy. Have you investigated their ability to close on time? Ask your Realtor for a referral and be sure to investigate and interview their recommendation.
- *Representativeness Heuristic*: Are you choosing a lender because they look like what you expect a lender to look like? Or did you do your due diligence and explore which one is likely to perform the best for your needs?
- *Anchoring*: How influenced are you by the Zestimate for a home? Are your expectations for the kind of home you should be able to afford driven by some past experience?
- *Confirmation Bias*: Are you avoiding getting pre-approved because you already know what the lender is going to say?
- *Anchoring/Representativeness/Availability*: Are you clear that what people do on TV is not real?

Points to Remember

- Buying a home is a journey. The more patience you have, the better the outcome will typically be for you.
- Find the right lender. Ideally, it will be a company that specializes in mortgages and has a track record of performing in partnership with your Realtor.
- Pre-qualification provides only a rough estimate of what you can afford in a house. It can be helpful at the start of the process, but it's not the whole story.

- Pre-approval is where the rubber meets the road in terms of what you can afford. Ideally, you should pursue pre-approval at the very start, even if you're not looking to buy for a year or more.
- In a competitive market, you won't be able to make an offer until you're pre-approved therefor, any good real estate agent, in that kind of market, won't even take you shopping for houses until you've done that work.
- Once you're pre-approved and know how much you can afford, it's time to list the amenities (size, location, style, etc.) that you want in a house and share that information with a Realtor.
- A good agent will then share with you the locations of properties that fit your budget and wish list before you ever head out to an open house or to visit a property.
- The pre-shopping consultation is the time for you to get grounded about what's available and how much you can afford. This is when you need to align your expectations with reality.
- Every house is a money pit, so don't overspend.

Chapter Eight:

Shopping and Finding

"Whoever said money can't buy happiness simply didn't know where to go shopping."

– Bo Derek

Now that you've covered your "pre's" and gotten your initial questions answered – your "pre's and q's" if you will (I couldn't resist) – you're now, hopefully, grounded in reality and ready to shop.

If you haven't noticed, almost everything in this book is an attempt to steer you away from using your gut feelings when buying or selling your home. The overall premise of the book is your instincts tend to be irrational and will cost you money. I generally assert using a more rational, data-driven approach will serve you better than going with your gut. That's clear by now, yes?

Okay. Ready? In this step (and perhaps only in this step), using your gut makes all the difference. Boots-on-the-ground, standing in the driveway of a particular house, you'll immediately get a feeling if this could be your home. You'll open the door and you'll just "know" it's your home. Likewise, there will be other properties you pull up to and won't even need to get out of the car because you know it isn't your home. That's how this phase of the process works.

In the information that follows, I'll point to some shortcuts and biases that make the process harder and more stressful than it needs to be. However, the actual decision that any given house is your next home is almost entirely one of feeling, and you need have little rationality about it. I don't mean you should fall in love with a house that creates a three-hour commute each way or is in some other way impractical. But I can tell you in every case, with every home I've ever sold, it's the same – the buyers knew right away this was it; this could be their home. There wasn't a lot of rationalizing they needed to do. When something fits, you know it. In fact, taking a more rational approach in every other step of the process creates the probability that when you find something that fits, you'll have the odds on your side to seal the deal and get the house you want.

This boots-on-the-ground phase can take place both with your Realtor and on your own. Often people aren't sure what neighborhood is right or are unsure exactly what they're looking for. That's fine. That's what this phase is all about. Seeing what's available. Standing in a house is different than seeing the pictures on Zillow. Driving a neighborhood is different than measuring the commute with Google maps. While I've shown, and sold, out-of-town clients houses via live video, that's an exception. The vast majority of people want to see the house they buy in person before buying it.

While 3D video walk throughs and virtual reality headsets are here now, there's little substitute to being in a house to know what it's like. What does a 1,200-square-foot house feel like? Is there enough space? How does the ceiling height work for you? What does the neighborhood feel like? Like I said, I've been with clients who – when we've pulled up the curb – tell me to "keep driving." Having seen it live, it's clear to them that it's not the house for them. They can't see themselves living there so why bother getting out of the car.

It's rare that it takes people more than a few minutes to determine whether or not they can live in a particular house. I'll say it again – in this step, gut reaction counts! A house is not something you should have to talk your spouse into liking as much as you do, nor should you settle for something you need to be talked into.

If you're considering many neighborhoods, try using the "brunching" method of house hunting. That's where you pick a neighborhood you're interested in, head over there for brunch on a Sunday and get a feel for the area. After brunch, you can hit some open houses of homes in your price range. This gives an easy, casual way to see if an area has the right vibe... and besides, who isn't looking for an excuse to brunch?

If you have a neighborhood picked based on commute, schools, proximity to recreational spaces, etc., then it's simpler. You know how much you can spend and where you want to be, so it's a question of seeing what's available.

One Man Gathers What Another Man Spills

Finding the right home could happen after just seeing a few homes or it could take over a year. It depends on your flexibility, the market conditions, and the quality of the Realtor you choose. Keep in mind, the marketplace is made up of people selling houses they no longer want or need. There's no guarantee a house exists with all your first round criteria, much less is being sold at a price you can afford at this precise time. Patience, being flexible, and keeping a realistic set of expectations are the key to happiness in most things – real estate being no exception. If you go through every house that's currently for sale that fits your criteria, without finding the right house, you'll need to either change your criteria or sit and wait for more to come to market.

TV Problems

Are you a fan of HGTV and the slew of home flipping/remodeling shows? As I already mentioned, these might leave you with a skewed picture of what it takes to turn a run-down house into something livable. *Availability* is directly correlated to vividness, and these shows are good at being vivid. The way these shows turn a house that's on the verge of being condemned into something you'd see on the cover of *Better Homes and Gardens* – in 60 minutes can create a problem for you.

In reality (not reality TV), buying a foreclosed house and turning it into something you'd love, takes more than what these shows might lead you to believe. Be careful: Unless you're already handy with a hammer, watching people on TV transform their house doesn't prepare you to do so. Thinking otherwise is the result of the shortcut created by the *Availability Heuristic.*

Anchoring can come into play when a house, early in the buying process, gets away. Now, every house is compared to that one. Similarly, a house from early in a person's life can become the reference point for all other houses. This makes shopping difficult. The value of the house is no longer considered relative to the values of other houses available now but against the value of the houses only *anchored* in the mind. It's very hard to compete with a memory.

The last shortcut worth mentioning here is *Prospect Theory*. The fear of loss, and our actions when we're afraid of losing something, can be a very costly shortcut if not managed. I've seen people offer more than they intended and take larger risks when they think there's a chance they might lose a house they like. In a competitive market, the risk of not being able to get the house you want is real, and *Prospect Theory* dictates you will risk more when the threat of loss is present. This may be exploited by either agent. A good listing agent, out to fulfill his or her fiduciary responsibility to bring the most money to a seller, is doing their job by creating a fear of loss in the buyers. A strong buyer's agent, however, will analyze the actual risk and guide a buyer to not get sucked into a situation that will later be regretted.

Avoid Being Shortchanged: Shortcuts to Watch For

- *Availability Heuristic*: The proliferation of reality shows on HGTV can fictitiously lead you to believe that flipping or renovating a property is well within your skill set.
- *Anchoring*: Perhaps a house you saw earlier in the buying process creates an unrealistic *anchor* against which you judge all other properties. A house from your past can also create an *anchor*.
- *Prospect Theory*: The seller or their agent will be quick to dangle the fear of loss in front of you knowing you'll risk more to avoid it!

Points to Remember

- Only in the shopping phase of the buying process should you rely on your gut instincts. In fact, it's critical that the house *feel* like it could be your home.
- Your relationship with reality dictates how stressful or frustrating house shopping will be. Patience, flexibility, and realistic expectations will help get you through.
- Shopping is the boots-on-the-ground part of the process. Love it or hate it, seeing houses in person is the best way to get a sense of how the size (now that you're in it and walking around) suits you and whether the neighborhood (despite any statistics on paper) meets your needs.

Chapter Nine:

You Found It! Now What?

"It doesn't matter which side of the fence you get off on some-times. What matters most is getting off. You cannot make progress without making decisions."

– Jim Rohn

Whether it's the second house you see during the shopping phase or you've been shopping for months, here you are. You've found it! Or, said accurately, you found one that could turn out to be it. This place has what you're looking for in terms of size and amenities, it's in the right neighborhood, and within your budget. Yay! You might even be popping open the champagne soon (especially if your search was a long one). Great. Now what?

While I remain clear that the selection process is the right time to engage your emotions (i.e., trust your gut), it's also not the time to throw logic and reason out the door.

Before you get emotionally attached to the house, there's a lot of work to do on the deal. While it's important that you're committed when making the choice, it's critical that you don't get attached. Not easy, I know. But that's part of the job of your Realtor – to keep you interested enough to make the offer, but not so attached that you couldn't walk away and find something else if needed. This is why it's so critical you find a Realtor you can trust. Not an impartial observer, but someone who considers it their job to make sure you get the best house, at the best price. This is where calling references will have made a difference. Hiring someone you found at an open house or because they offered a discount could bite you hard in this phase.

Before you commit to this house, I consider it a best practice to list all of its shortcomings. We use a checklist we stole from another great agent team in our office (thank you, Black and Pickett). They've generously allowed me to offer you a download of the sheet they use at www.rationalrealestate.pro/null. You'll see it has every possible feature listed and an opportunity to mark if any deficiencies in those areas are either "curable" or "incurable." Curable issues are things like the water heater is old, the roof needs work, the plumbing needs updating, etc. Incurable issues include where it's located (i.e., the neighborhood, school district, on a busy street), its orientation on the lot, etc.

Operating this way will put you, the buyer, at a strategic advantage as it puts the house in the position of needing to prove itself worth buying. This is the due diligence required by the CEO of any large company when looking at the single largest purchase that business will ever make. Don't justify shortcutting this step because you fell in love with some aspects of the house. Even if it is your "dream home," you still need to examine all the "warts" so you know what you're getting yourself into.

Once the house proves itself worthy of writing an offer, then you can start to think about price. While we'll do a deeper dive on this in the next chapter, to get the ball rolling, you can start by asking, "Is it worth the asking price to me?"

Notice, I didn't say, "Is it worth the asking price?" I said, "Is it worth the asking price **to me**?" Houses are not worth anything until someone is willing to pay for them. It's worth, to you, is what you say it's worth. Sure, other houses of comparable size, condition, location, etc. can inform you as to what others think it might be worth to them, but that's still not the same as what it's worth to you. Maybe you're moving in a very tight time frame and must get a house immediately. That could make it worth more to you than the next guy. Suppose the next guy feels it's worth 20 percent more than the asking price. Well, then that's what it's worth to them. Are they overpaying? Not if they think it's worth it to them. Would it be overpaying for you to get in a bidding war and pay 25 percent more? Maybe, maybe not. It's your call.

Current market conditions play a significant role at this point. The likelihood of other suitable houses being available in your time frame can change the perception of value. This all should have been detailed in your pre-shopping consultation and now its importance will be obvious.

This idea, that there is no "true value" and there is no "right" answer, will keep coming up throughout this book. You will, at every step, be best served by ceasing the search for *the right answers* and to look for answers that are *right for you.*

We'll keep looking a price as we go through the steps as price, value, and money in general all are fertile ground for shortcuts to come into play.

Anchoring and the ***Endowment Effect*** have serious implications on maintaining a rational thought process at this point. Many times, and for many reasons, a client will fall in love with a house and, like most instances involving love, will lose all sense of rationality. Do I need to make a case for the stupid things love has made you do? When buying a house, it's simple, if not always easy to avoid. It's a matter of being aware of your own mental shortcuts.

The potential problems begin when buyers start to see themselves living in the house in question. The longer this happens, the more vividly this house matches prior ***anchors*** and the images of what they want their home to look and feel like, the harder it becomes to keep operating rationally. I get into more arguments with buyers about ***Anchoring*** than any other topic. I've even lost clients because they felt I kept talking them out of buying houses they liked too many times. People, of any age, don't like to be told they shouldn't have what their heart desires. This is one more reason to hire someone to represent you. Someone needs to drive you home when you're drunk on love.

Given house hunting is often a team sport, with most home-owners being a couple or family unit, it's not uncommon for one person to be on one side of the impact of the *Endowment Effect* and the other to be situated on the flip side. For example, one person is not seeing themselves as the owner yet (therefore placing a lower value on the house) while the other person is already figuring out what color the room needs to be to match the couch and, given they experience living in the house already, value the home more highly. Those differences are always fun for your Realtor to navigate.

The next steps in the process – valuing the home, writing the offer, negotiating the deal, and the steps leading up to having your offer accepted by the seller – all need to happen only after all parties on the buy side are on the same page. Like every other partnership, deals don't go well when one party is excited to get started but the other is getting ready to leave. There needs to be alignment here and that includes between the buyers and their agent. When everyone is on the same page, you can move to the next steps.

> **Key Point:** Bottom line here: You need to walk the line between being interested enough (in love enough) with the home to be willing to write the offer and own it, but not so in love with it that you lose your perspective about its value to you compared to what else is on the market. This is neither simple nor is it easy, but with a skilled professional at your side and some self-awareness, you'll be fine.

Avoid Being Shortchanged: Shortcuts to Watch For

- *Anchoring*: You must be committed to the home enough to write an offer but not so **anchored** that you can't walk away if the deal turns sour at some point and is no longer in your best interest.
- *Endowment Effect*: If you start to envision yourself too clearly living in the house and thinking of it as "your home," you will begin to value it more highly. Don't lose your ability to make a rational decision about your offer and what you are willing to pay.

Points to Remember

- Make a case against every house, forcing the house to prove itself to you. It's a big decision, so no shortcuts.
- To determine this house's value, you must know the various aspects and nuances of the current market, starting with whether it's currently a buyer's or seller's market. This should have been covered with you during your pre- shopping consultation.
- All parties need to be on the same page before writing an offer.
- Give your agent the keys, so they can help steer you away from houses you may love "too much."

Chapter Ten:

Making an Offer

"Everything is negotiable. Whether or not the negotiation is easy is another thing."

– Carrie Fisher

If you've found your future home and you want to write a winning offer, you need to think like a seller and understand the market conditions. An intelligent and competitive offer will be one that reflects a deep understanding of what the seller wants and what's happening around you. Hiring that guy with lots of web site stars, or the friendly lady from the open house, or that company that said they'd give you $2,000 back might not prove to be the best move.

Both you and your agent need to understand that supply and demand is not just a good idea, it's the law. The offer you write needs to be consistent with what the market demands. High demand but little supply (aka a seller's market), creates higher prices and more concessions from buyers. When there's more supply but little demand (aka a buyer's market), prices go down and concessions can be asked of sellers.

Remember, real estate is hyperlocal. There can be, and usually are, varying market conditions across the country, state, and sometimes down to the neighborhood or block. Even within a city during the strongest seller's market in 15 years, we find areas where homes are still available under asking price. If you interviewed well, you should have uncovered this information and picked someone who can do this, too.

When deciding how much to offer remember that market conditions do shift. They don't, however, usually shift in a radical way overnight. If it's a seller's market when you started shopping then, unless your agent advises you that it's starting to trend in the opposite direction, it means you'll have to face the reality of buying under those market conditions. Waiting this out means thinking in terms of years for it to change. On the other hand, if you have the luxury of a buyer's market, you'll also likely have the bonus of taking your time on your decision and shopping around. That said, neither is a given: A seller's market doesn't necessarily mean that you'll end up paying above asking price and a buyer's market doesn't guarantee the house you want won't be sold out from under you while you're considering it.

Real estate in the U.S. has tended to run in seven- to ten-year cycles, depending on the economist you ask. Again, this is hyperlocal. In 2017, we're seeing some areas of the country that have just now gotten back to pre-crash values while other areas are already shifting into a down trend. Finding a Realtor you can consider to be your local economist of choice is a smart investment of time.

With the best possible information available about the local economic conditions, you now enter the arena to write an offer on a house you want. Given the background work you've done so far, you should already be clear on the type and strength of the market. The answers to the following questions should've been clear to you before you ever went to see the first house on your list:

- Will you need to write an offer quickly?
- Is a pre-inspection going to be required?
- Is there a set date on which the sellers will be reviewing offers?
- How long has the house been on the market?

- How long are homes like this staying on the market?
- Is it priced above, below, or right at predictable market value?
- Is it likely to gather multiple offers or do you have room to negotiate a lower price?

The answers to each of these questions represent a different scenario about how the transaction might play out. You'll need to know how to deal with each one because each one impacts the type of offer you're going to write and how you're going to negotiate that offer.

> **Side Note:** It's typical that home inspections occur later in the process, so we'll cover them in a later chapter. But in certain instances, you could end up with an inspection needed at this point (a pre-inspection). If this is the case in your market, your agent will need to create a plan around that.

The most important factor in this step is knowing whether you're dealing with a buyer's market or a seller's market and the relative "temperature" of either. You need to know who, by virtue of the market conditions, has the leverage in this initial phase of the negotiation. If you're wondering why it's critical for you to interview to find the best buyer's agent to represent you, this is it. You aren't hiring them to search Zillow for you. With the amount of data available to the consumer about houses for sale, the value an agent adds isn't usually in finding the right home. It's more likely found in their ability to read the current market and the motivations of each party. An agent's job is to put together a compelling offer that serves the best interest of their client while also occurring as a win for the other party.

You'll want someone who can read the market and its fluctuations and then write and negotiate an offer consistent with those conditions. This is why choosing your cousin's husband's best friend's brother because he comes to mind first (i.e., the *Availability Heuristic* at play) is akin to total insanity.

As a listing agent, I've seen more than a few offers from agents who clearly had no clue what was happening in the market. This tells me their client never interviewed them or, if they did, failed to understand and ask the right questions. The result? Their client lost out on the property or ended up paying way too much. I've been on the receiving end of offers, made by discount brokers, who turned over to me twice what they purported to be saving their client. Turns out they weren't offering a discount because they were extra nice guys. They offered a discount because nobody would hire them if they knew what kind of results they produced.

There are many factors, elements, and contingencies that go into writing an offer that you'd do well to understand. While it's a little too detailed to define each of these aspects here (not mention they differ from state to state), I do recommend you spend some time researching these terms on your own. If you're interested, I've developed training videos for some of the most common aspects that can be accessed at www.rationalrealestate.pro/offers.

The smartest move would be to go through a sample contract far ahead of needing to sign one. In Washington State, they run 20 to 30 pages long, so there's some reading for sure. Ask your agent about anything unclear to you. Let them explain it until you're satisfied that you know what's going on. Remember: You're the CEO. They work for you, and you're the one who will deal with the consequences of this purchase every day. Your agent, no matter how good, will get paid and move on. It's up to you to make sure you're clear about everything at all times. Only choose an agent who understands that.

In addition to all the typical legalese, you'll also need to cover the specifics about the property in the offer. For example, will the appliances convey and be part of the deal? What about window treatments? How about the flat screen TV mounts? It's possible some will and some won't. Love the drapes in the living room? Unless you spell out in your offer that you want them to stay, they may not, and you'll be disappointed on move-in day. That swing set in the backyard that your kids were excited about when you saw the house? Ditto. It may need to be spelled out with the offer.

With all that in the background, you now must come up with the amount you are willing to offer and the terms with which you are willing to offer it. This is a back-and-forth dialogue with your agent, and at the end of it, you must be comfortable with what you come up with. (Keep in mind that fear and excitement are emotions with similar manifestations, so "comfortable" might not be the right word.)

To arrive at this point in the most rational way, you'll need to watch for a few shortcuts that are likely to interfere. Since you'll be putting money at stake, you should be on high alert for the impact of **Prospect Theory**, **Anchoring** and the **Endowment Effect**.

We reviewed the **Endowment Effect** previously when selecting this house as one worthy of writing an offer on. How attached have you already become? Notice your thoughts here. Are you a newlywed and already picturing the grandkids visiting? You might be a little too attached at this point and should definitely be wary of the **Endowment Effect** coloring your perception of value.

Without a doubt, the price the seller is using as the starting point is an **anchor** but so might be the price for which you sold a previous house. I've been with clients who have sold a house in a market that was much less expensive than the market where they were buying. The amount of money they sold their 3,000-square-foot split level in Kansas couldn't buy them a 1,000-square-foot condo in Seattle. The degree to which they had their old home's value *anchored* as "what homes are worth" was the degree to which they were upset. This happens in reverse when people move from a more expensive market to a less expensive one. In that case, people are delighted with how much more house they can buy for the same money. In either case, the value of a home is being referenced against an *anchor* from another market. Not a useful practice in determining the value of this particular home in this particular market.

I suspect I'm not the only Realtor who's had to deal with a client whose expectations of the market and home values were set in how prices played out the last time they sold. It's also not uncommon to meet buyers who've heard a family member or friend talk about the deal they got recently in some neighborhood (or city or state) that we aren't shopping in. Never mind that these situations could not be less relevant, these stories stick in the mind and shape their view of how the market they are looking in "should" behave. These are the *Availability* and *Anchoring* shortcuts at work.

The constant bombardment of input from TV compounds the issue. Everything from news programming to reality TV home shows are creating the thoughts that are *available* to you.

Sometimes perceived value is shaped in surprising ways. For example, imagine you're shopping in a strong seller's market where houses are selling in a few days and for multiple offers over their asking price. One morning your agent presents you with a house that meets many of your criteria, in an area of town that's pretty close to where you've been looking. With many criteria met and after looking at it in person, you find it does fit in many ways. But this home has been on the market for three times as long as other homes and has had one price drop. Are you more likely to think, "Oh good, what a bargain!" or "What's wrong with this place?" Almost all buyers think the latter.

In the above example, there may, in fact, be some fatal flaw with the house that other buyers keep noticing and walking away from. But it could also be listed by a terrible agent, overpriced and under-marketed. For now, focus on your reaction. Does it indicate someone operating on automatic inside a shortcut? Are you willing to have found a needle in a haystack? Under the pressure of putting your life savings into a home like that, you'll need to discover the answer for yourself.

At the end of the day, you and your agent will need to come up with a price and terms and submit an offer that, if accepted, will make you happy. *This is the critical piece of negotiating.* You must have a price at or below which, if accepted, you'd be happy and above which you'd be happy for the person who thought it was worth that much (but it won't be you). This is your "walk away" point. Don't write an offer without being clear on that number, or you open yourself up to being put in a situation you'll regret. That number should reflect all the rational thought you can muster, reflect the market conditions (supply and demand), and be within a range that you'll be comfortable writing a check every month. Remember: no deal is better than a bad deal.

Offer Rejection

The next chapters will cover everything that follows having your offer accepted, but let's look at the other side of that coin. What happens if your offer is rejected? In most cases, an unacceptable offer will be met with a counter offer. This leaves you inside a negotiation, which, if you hired well, should be no problem. A good agent will be prepared for a counter offer.

However, the negotiations could produce no agreement or you're offer could simply be outright rejected. In a seller's market, this most likely means you lost the home to another buyer who paid more or had better terms. But whether you're in a buyer's or a seller's market, your offer could always be rejected and this is worth examining.

Be careful and notice how you react to being rejected. ***Prospect Theory*** suggests you're more likely to start taking risks if you now approach the process from the vantage point of avoiding the next loss. Get rejected too many times and the ***Availability Heuristic*** could begin to wear down your will and leave you resigned that you'll never find your place. While it might just be positive thinking, I always ask my clients to think of finding their home like they think about finding their spouse – you might have had some heart-breaking relationships in the past, but each one, in its own way, helped pave the way for you to find the one you're with right now. Awwwwwwww....

When market conditions are tight, with multiple buyers writing offers, bidding wars can break out for each house sold. There's only one house and multiple buyers and, well, you can do that math. When you find yourself in a multiple-offer situation, here are three things you can do to avoid having your offer rejected.

First, know the game you're in. It could be, based on market conditions, that if your top dollar amount is $500,000 that you can't even look at houses listed above $400,000. If nothing in the area you're shopping is going less than $100,000 over asking price, it doesn't make sense to start higher. It seems crazy but some markets are like that. In a multiple-offer situation, I usually think of each offer representing about a three to five percent increase in the price over the asking price. That means on a house in a hot market listed at $500,000 with three offers on it, I'd expect it sell for between $550,000 to 575,000. True in every case? Nope. But it's close enough that if my client was unwilling to pay more than $525,000, I wouldn't recommend that they pay money to have the home pre-inspected if I knew of three other offers already. Do your homework and start at the right price.

Know where you're buying. Spend your time wisely, so you're not putting in offers that you have little chance of winning!

Second, pick the right lender. We covered this earlier, and now is when choosing the right lender can come home to work in your favor and choosing the wrong lender will work against you. As soon as you place an offer, contact your lender (or have your agent do it) and have them call the listing agent for the property. Why? You want the lender to "talk you up" to the listing agent, reiterating your pre-approval and credit worthiness.

Consider this scenario on a house with multiple offers: The listing agent gets a call from a lender, "Hello, I understand that the Smiths put in an offer on your listing, and I want you to know that I personally have been working with them for the past several months. They're fantastic and are completely qualified for this loan. I have absolutely no question about this loan going through, and in fact, it's already gone through underwriting. I'm happy to answer any questions you may have."

It's standard practice for good listing agents to call every lender prior to presenting offers to the seller. By having your lender call the agent first, you stand out. You've made the agent's job easier. It's a little thing, but do enough little things right and the big things fall your way. Plus, if your competition's lender makes this call to the listing agent and yours does not, well, you might stand out, but not in the way you want.

This is one more reason I cautioned you against picking a big bank as your mortgage lender when you were getting pre-qualified. Using a national bank, or worse, some internet-based lender, for your loan, will place you at a disadvantage compared to buyers using a local lender. By using a local lender, you're greasing the wheels toward both getting your mortgage and – most importantly – getting the house! A good listing agent will steer their seller toward the buyer who is best positioned to close the deal quickly and on time. In fact, when I'm the listing agent and my clients ask which buyer they should select, I recommend the one with the local lender almost every time! Using the right lender and having that lender call on your behalf can give you a solid competitive edge.

Third, know that your agent has a track record of winning in multiple-offer situations. How can you know this? Based on the interview you conducted before you even agreed to have them represent you. Can they show you their track record? Can they give you contact information for previous clients they successfully represented in multiple-offer situations? It's a simple question to ask them: "So, in recent multiple-offer situations, how have you done? Can I have the names of those clients, so I can talk to them about their experience?"

It's not complicated, but don't drop the ball on following up on the referrals. "Hey, how was it to work with Bob? Did you get the house you wanted? Was it a good experience? Would you do it again?" Talk to them!

Why is this so important? Because doing this, you'll know the Realtor you chose has a demonstrated strategy that works. If you don't want to spin your wheels, waste your time, or risk disappointment in losing out on the house you want, this is critical. Know the skills of the agent representing you... and don't learn they don't have them when it's time to write and negotiate the offer!

These three tips aren't rocket science, and they won't guarantee that you'll get the house, but they will indeed give you an edge, and that's exactly what you'll need when buying in a seller's market.

Avoid Being Shortchanged: Shortcuts to Watch For

- *Anchoring Heuristic*: The seller's asking price creates an **anchor**, but be aware of the **anchors** created by your experience in other geographic markets and/or your own history.
- *Prospect Theory*: Because the process involves a lot of money, you must be cognizant of having a greater sensitivity to loss than to gain. You might take larger and larger risks on the houses you like after you lose out on the first one.
- *Availability Heuristic:* Rejection, especially multiple rejected offers, can wear you down and lead you to believe that you will never find the right house. The news, and reality TV, all shape what's *available* in your mind to think. Stay out here, in the market, and avoid knee-jerk reactions and automatic thinking.

Points to Remember

- Real estate is hyperlocal, and you should be aware (as should your agent!) of the conditions in which you are shopping.
- Whether it's a buyer's or seller's market, your offer should reflect the market conditions; otherwise, you're wasting your time and your money.
- Learn about the market conditions under which you will be placing an offer long before you get to that phase of the process.
- Review a sample contract before you're faced with reviewing an actual one. This type of education and homework will serve you well.

- Your agent earns their money by understanding how to put together an offer and negotiating the deal for you... much more so than by locating and showing houses for sale.
- Be very clear about your "walk away" point and use what you know about shortcuts to avoid getting stuck in a deal that isn't in your best interest.
- There are three things you can do to avoid rejection: know the game you're in, pick the right lender, and select an agent with a winning track record in multiple-offer situations.

Chapter Eleven:

Acceptance!

"Coming together is a beginning; keeping together is progress; working together is success."

– Henry Ford

Your offer was accepted! Hallelujah. High-fives all around and a champagne toast **might** be in your future.

Ah, but I can hear you now, "Wait. What? Might be in my future? Why wouldn't it be? The offer was accepted!" Well, reaching this phase doesn't mean you're done. Better save that champagne for closing day. When you're "mutual," you're protected from someone else coming in and making an offer. However, it's important to keep in mind that there are still many, many ways for this deal to fall apart.

You will hear this phase referred to as "pending" or "being mutual" or "being under contract." All mean the same thing. You have a contract that has been mutually agreed to and is pending the completion of certain items. This does not guarantee the deal is going to go through. If any of the called for items that are pending completion are not completed, there is no deal.

Let's look at what still needs to be accomplished, what's still pending completion, and what next steps each brings with it.

You've written an offer and the other side accepted it, so now you're mutually contracted to perform certain tasks. This ends with your obligation to close on a specified date and their obligation to turn over the house to you on a specific date.

Your agent should have reviewed with you, specific to your locale, all the contingencies in place so you know exactly what they are and their impact. Your agent should also have given you a timeline in which the next steps are laid out. What follows is a 10,000-foot overview of the most common contingencies and timelines. In the chapters that follow, I'll do a deeper dive on some of these, as each presents its own opportunity for you to choose to operate rationally (or irrationally). Please make certain you take the time with your agent to review and understand the particulars required by your city and state.

The very first performance you are counted on for is delivering your earnest money to escrow. While the exact procedure for this varies with locality, the principle is the same. You are putting money up to assure you are, in fact, "earnest" about buying this property. You are, in essence, saying that if you fail to perform in any of the expected ways, the seller can keep this deposit. If you follow through with everything you promise this money is returned to you (generally people use this as part of their down payment). The contingencies you have in the contract are there, ostensibly, to protect you from losing this earnest money. If you fail to deliver the earnest money in the specified time (usually 48 hours), the deal is null and void. In a very real way as soon as both parties have signed the contract, the countdown starts and you need to stay on timeline.

Next, if you have a finance contingency, the lender will need to start their process in order to provide the money for the loan by the closing date. This contingency protects you from losing your earnest money by allowing you a legal "out" should the lender fail to produce the loan as promised.

The lender will start by getting an appraisal, a professional, third-party opinion of the property. No lender will give you a mortgage for an amount higher than what it appraises for. To determine the appraised value, they'll call for an independent appraiser to view the property and confirm the home was worth what you paid. More on this step later.

Sometimes people confuse appraisal with assessments. Appraisals are used by banks to approve loans. Assessments are used by local governments to determine taxes. These numbers are almost always different and, for your purposes at this point in securing a loan for the property, unrelated.

Another typical contingency allows for a home inspection. (Again, much more on this in the next chapter.) This contingency allows you to hire, at your expense, someone to inspect the home for deficiencies. You can expect to have seven to ten days after you and the seller have reached an agreement to execute this process. The specifics of how and when this is done are detailed in your contract. At the heart of it, this contingency should allow you to cancel the deal for any reason based on what the inspector finds. It does not require the seller to fix anything the inspection uncovers. But should they decline to do so, you can cancel the deal and get your earnest money back.

A title contingency demands the seller present a clean and clear title to the property as part of their performance. As the buyer, you must be assured that there aren't any liens on the property that might negate the ability for it to transfer to a new owner or for which you could become responsible.

Your agent and your lender have to work in tandem on your behalf – sort of a pilot/co-pilot relationship –bringing the deal to closing. This is yet another reason to use the lender your Realtor referred (or a Realtor your lender referred). When you get a referral for one from the other, you'll know that these two professionals have worked together previously. Their ability to work together is necessary to bring the deal to a successful completion. If for some reason your Realtor and lender have not worked together previously, it's important that they establish a relationship and are on the same page working on your behalf. Unfortunately, I've seen a lot of deals scuttled because the Realtor and lender failed to work together – each one thought the other was handling certain details, but in reality, neither was.

While every state differs, you can expect the chapters that follow to outline the normal steps you'll need to take. Please be sure to confirm the specifics with your agent. Miss a deadline anywhere along the way, and you may not get the house. Worse, you may be liable for damages, so don't assume anything. Smart CEOs make it their job to understand what and when everything is to happen.

Avoid Being Shortchanged: Shortcuts to Watch For

In the chapters that follow, we'll continue to point out the short-cuts most likely to interfere with closing on your new home. Anything that can cloud your better judgment as you make decisions along the path to getting your keys will be called out.

Time is of the essence at this stage. Your ability to act quickly, decisively, and rationally will payoff down the road, as certainly as hesitating and operating slowly or irrationally could cost you dearly.

Points to Remember

- Once your offer is accepted, you're now "mutual," and both parties have responsibilities and performances to carry out.
- There are specific contingencies in the agreement that must be met for a successful transaction.
- It is critical for you to understand each contingency and its impact as they provide you or the seller with an "out" if certain aspects of the transaction do not unfold as expected.

- Your Realtor and lender must have a good working relationship. In a perfect world, they'll already know each other and will have worked together before. A successful closing depends on their collaboration.
- As you get closer to closing on the home of your dreams, you must continue to be aware of these shortcuts. Don't let them derail your rational thinking at the time when you need it most.

Chapter Twelve:

You Get What You Inspect (Not What You Expect)

"Education is learning what you didn't even know you didn't know."

– Daniel Boorstein

A home inspection is your chance to get a thorough education in the quality and condition of the most expensive thing you are ever going to buy. If there are any fatal, hidden problems, now is when you'll want to uncover them.

If you'll recall, I mentioned in Chapter 10: Making an Offer, that an inspection might be needed at that point – before you make the offer. But why would you, as the buyer, pay for an inspection (between $300 and $700) before you even knew you had an accepted offer? Here's the logic:

- If you don't do it before making an offer, you're going to need to do it after.
- If you do it after, you're going to need an inspection contingency allowing you out of the deal if you don't like what the inspection shows.
- Any contingency makes your offer weaker from the seller's perspective.

- Doing the inspection before you write the offer will let you feel comfortable enough with the condition of the house that you won't need to add that contingency to the offer.
- Thus, making your offer stronger than anyone else's offer that includes that contingency.

It's a big deal. In a multiple-offer situation, as soon as one of the potential buyers waives the inspection contingency, any other offer that includes one is, for all intents and purposes, not a viable offer anymore. In most cases, if your agent discovers another potential buyer has done a pre-inspection on a home you're looking at, you'll need to plan on doing one as well or you're going to have a hard time being competitive.

Happily, it's not typical to be in such a competitive market that pre-inspections are needed. That's why we're covering the process from perspective of what happens after you've had your offer accepted, as that is far more common.

The inspection contingency states that the offer depends on the property passing an inspection to your satisfaction. Whether or not it "meets your satisfaction" depends on your particular contract in terms of cancellation. Some states have a very, very broad definition of a satisfactory inspection. For example, in Washington State, if you don't like what the inspection report shows, without any other justification, you can get out of the deal and get your earnest money back. In some respects, it's a "get out of deal free" card. Read your contract before you sign, so you know what your contingency will allow for.

It's your responsibility as the buyer to schedule the inspection on the house and you'll need to do it within the timeframe spelled out in your contract. I recommend you hire a professional home inspector, which, if you don't have one, your agent should be able to recommend. It's important to note that you're responsible to pay for this service. Home inspections typically cost somewhere between $300 and $700 with most inspectors expecting payment at the time of the inspection. If possible, it's a good idea to be present and go through the home with the inspector. They'll be able to point out what they found and clarify your understanding of their report. This helps you get a better sense of the condition of the home and its mechanical workings.

Detailed and Thorough

Whether or not you're present during the inspection, the inspector will provide a detailed – and I do mean detailed – report of the deficiencies in the house. There could be 100 items marked as "deficient" on that report, but don't freak out. We're talking about a house with all its mechanical systems, doors, windows, etc., so there's a lot to cover.

Depending on the home's age, the report could show a lot of things that aren't quite right or flat out need repair. The report should include everything the inspector finds. To help you better understand the detail level of the inspection report, I've included a sample report for you at www.rationalrealestate.pro/inspection.

Everything comes up on this report... and it should! If you're a bit squeamish, you're in trouble. This report is going to list the details on those 100 different things that could be deemed deficient about the property. Brace yourself now and be prepared for it.

While you are touring the home with the inspector, be sure to ask anything you want to know about the house. Many inspectors have a background in building or construction and are knowledgeable about repair costs.

With any luck, most deficiencies will be minor, but it's possible there will be some things you consider major to contend with. While it's within your right to ask for repairs to things you were aware of when you wrote the offer, I think it's bad form to do so. You saw it when you wrote the offer; therefore, you and your agent should have included that in the price you offered. If there were no closet doors, and you knew there were no closet doors, your offer should be based on there being no closet doors. Going back now and asking for closet doors at this point seems to me to be negotiating in bad faith.

However, you will most likely have a long list of deficiencies that have come to light during the inspection. For these, you do have the right to say, "We will continue with this transaction if you fix the following...."

Here is where you can use your understanding of the typical shortcuts other people have to get what you want. My recommendation is for you to harness the power of *Framing* in your negotiation of the repairs. Suppose there are three or four items on the list you didn't know about and you want the seller to handle. They may or may not be deal killers, but you'd at least feel better about the deal if the seller dealt with them. No problem. Start your inspection response by pointing out the 100 deficiencies noted in the report. Then present a list of ten things that you want the seller to fix. The negotiating pitch is that there's a lot wrong with the house, but you're willing to move forward if they take care of just these ten.

If the seller's agent also knows how the game is played, they may come back and say, "Well, we're not going to address all ten things, but we'll take care of these five items on your list." Of course, you could get lucky and deal with a seller using a discount broker, or someone else lousy at negotiating, and they go ahead and repair, or give you a concession in price, to cover all ten. Congrats to you.

This is a brand new round of negotiations. You can cancel the deal at this point with no loss (other than the money it cost for the inspection). If the seller is unwilling to meet your demands, you can dissolve the contract. It's for this reason that offers without an inspection contingency are so much stronger than those with one. Even if there are multiple offers for the same amount, if one offer has waived the inspection contingency, I assure you, the seller is going to go with that offer. That buyer is effectively saying, "Here's our offer and we're not walking away because of anything we discover in the inspection later." It would be silly for the seller to choose otherwise.

That said, in most cases, the inspection comes after the offer is accepted. This means you'll have a lot of leverage. Once the house is off the market (as it has been since you went "mutual"), the seller is not going to want to put the house back up for sale. Take advantage of your position. Make sure your agent is sharp enough to negotiate the greatest number of repairs on your behalf. In the case of smaller, less critical but still deficient areas, the seller might be willing to offer a concession on price. The point is: it never hurts to ask.

Again, on the flip side, if you're in a seller's market and have done an inspection prior to writing the offer so you could waive the inspection contingency as part of the offer and position yourself as a more attractive buyer, you will, in all likelihood, not be asking for any improvements or repairs. You'll get the inspection report to know what it is you're buying and make your offer price based on that information.

To be clear: It's critical that you do an inspection at some point. Buying a house without an inspection is sort of a *"Warning Will Robinson! Danger!"* kind of risky thing to do. Yes, you'll be investing a couple hundred dollars to make the offer, and, yes, that's money you cannot recoup. But you'll have a greater, and in my view, necessary, education on what you'll need to fix in the house after you own it.

There are other inspections or feasibility tests that can also come into play at this point. These include a sewer scope, septic suitability tests, well testing, soil testing, etc. Ask your agent what tests make sense for the property you are looking at.

Sometimes the seller will have already done some of these and will provide the results, and for others, you will need to do them yourself. In fact, some savvy sellers provide a full inspection report up front to encourage multiple offers while taking the risk of a possible second negotiation off the table.

An inspection done by a licensed and bonded inspector, but paid for by the seller, creates an interesting opportunity for a buyer. You can choose to accept their inspection and make an offer that reflects the condition of the home as reported. Or you can choose to write your offer as if there had been no inspection, add an inspection contingency, and pay for your own.

Doing your own, in the face of the report you've already been provided, does create the situation I mentioned above. It might turn out to be unrealistic to expect that the seller will repair anything that the buyer knew about prior to writing the offer. Unless your inspector turns something up that is not listed in the inspection report you were provided prior to writing, you're unlikely to get additional concessions. The decision on how to proceed in this case is between you and your agent and is dependent on the condition of the house and the condition of the market.

I've had more than one buyer back out after reading the inspection report. When anything moves from dream to reality, we tend to see the defects we missed earlier. With a home purchase, you're handed a 25-page document with pictures and descriptions of every single one. If the buyer starts weighing the risks more heavily than the rewards, as **Prospect Theory** indicates we are likely to do, then there is a better than even chance the inspection report can sour the deal.

While I've already told you I approach the purchase of any home from the view that it's not worth buying, if we get to this stage, we don't want to be scared off by trivial or inexpensive problems. Every house has its physical deficiencies, new construction as well, so it's all about relative value and a rational assessment of the risks.

Rationally speaking, as I've said before, every home is a money pit. There's a never-ending list of improvements, upgrades and repairs to be done. The list you're holding from your inspector is likely to be thorough, and yet, it will be incomplete. There will be more coming, if not now, then soon. Count on that. But you can also count on a list like that coming for any house you look at. You and your agent should take a long hard look at the list and at the market to determine if this house represents a value at the price offered or if there is likely to be something better out there. Don't let your cognitive bias toward loss avoidance sway you toward or away from the house.

Less frequently, people have had some past, horrible experience with a remodel or some specific problem from a past home, and the *Availability Heuristic* comes into play. In fact, more often than having a horrible experience from the past, I find people have some image implanted from an HGTV reality show, and they are inappropriately emboldened to take on too big of a project for their own particular skills. Remember when I said every home is a money pit? Well, some are bigger than others, and if you walk into a foreclosed home that's been on the market for months thinking you've found a bargain that every other investor and home flipper has missed, think again.

Both the irrational fear from a past remodel or the irrational confidence instilled from "reality" TV are a function of the *Availability Heuristic*. Running into either will wind up costing you so slow down, breathe, and take the time to create a rational plan.

Avoid Being Shortchanged: Shortcuts to Watch For

- *Framing:* Use this heuristic to your advantage during the second negotiation that occurs after the inspection report is delivered.

- **Prospect Theory:** Don't let fear of loss, which could be instilled based on the inspection report, cause you to back away from what might be the right house for you. Every property will have its issues.
- **Anchoring:** Conversely, be sure to avoid being so **anchored** to the property that you ignore giant red flags that the inspection may uncover.
- **Availability:** Just because you see it repeatedly on HGTV doesn't mean that renovations are easy or are something you can realistically handle.

Points to Remember

- This house is going to be the most expensive thing you purchase, so don't cut corners with the inspection. Use a qualified, licensed home inspector.
- Be prepared for a very detailed report that may contain 100 to 150 items listed as deficient with the property. Don't panic.
- When your offer is contingent on the inspection, you can walk away and cancel the contract (with return of your earnest money), or you can work to renegotiate with the seller regarding making needed repairs.
- Renegotiating at this point gives you a lot of leverage now because most sellers will not want to place the house back on the market.
- In a seller's market, you might need to have the inspection done prior to making an offer, so you'll be aware of the property's deficiencies beforehand but can avoid having your offer contingent on the results.

Chapter Thirteen:

Appraisals

"A nickel ain't worth a dime anymore."

– Yogi Berra

Your dream home has passed your inspection! Whether you conducted a pre-offer inspection or did it as a contingency with your offer and renegotiated any needed repairs, you've successfully negotiated the waiver of the inspection contingency and you're ready for the next step. Now you're on to the appraisal process.

Like the home inspection, you're responsible for the cost of the appraisal. The expense will be similar to that of the inspection; however, you have far less say about this part of the process. Since the housing market collapse in 2007, neither you nor your lender can talk to the appraiser prior to appraisal.

The appraiser will walk through the house and report what they can see with the naked eye. They're not privy to the inspection report, nor will they see the seller's disclosure form. If there happens to be a roof leak that's only apparent in the attic space, the appraiser is probably not going to know about it. (A leak that's causing a water stain on the living room ceiling is another matter.)

After a quick walk through they'll return to their office and pull the "comps" (comparables) of similar properties and adjust for the size and age of the property as well as the neighborhood, and tell the lender their opinion of the value of the house.

In essence, the lender is looking to confirm the house is worth the amount they are lending you.

> **Key Point:** You wouldn't want to spend the money for the appraisal until the house has been inspected. If the house doesn't pass your inspection, you don't need the appraisal. Be certain that if your Realtor is calling for the appraisal before the inspection is complete, you're crystal clear as to what their thinking is about doing so. Paying for something you may not need is silly.

The appraiser is looking to come up with a value they feel a typical buyer would pay for the property that's supported by recent sales. In other words, they're looking for the market value of the home. The appraiser gets to choose which closed sales (comps) to use, and when comparing them there are factors that are not subjective in the comparison (such as the number of bedrooms and bathrooms) and there are factors that are subjective (such as the value of a view, the quality of construction, added value of landscaping, finished basement quality, etc.).

Honestly, 90 times out of 100, the value of the home comes in at what you paid for it. The market value of the house is what you paid for it because you are the market. If there were 11 offers and it drove the price well past asking, that could be said to be the new market price. While it doesn't mean the bank will always validate it, the price you paid is market value.

However, if the appraisal doesn't come in "at value," (e.g., you paid $500,000 but the appraisal says it's worth $450,000), it means the lender is only cutting you a check based on $450,000. If that should happen, you'll be happy that your Realtor made sure you had a suitable finance contingency in place that allows you to renegotiate the price or annul the deal.

As the inspection contingency protects you from problems of a physical nature uncovered after the price has been agreed upon, a finance contingency protects you from problems with your financing. Under-appraisal is one such possible problem, and you need to make certain your contract has such a protection in it. Without that protection, you'd need to come up with the full amount of the difference between the accepted price and the appraised price, in this example $50,000.

In the above scenario, with a finance contingency in place, one of four things will need to happen:

1. You could make up the difference, so the seller gets the full amount you offered, or
2. You could negotiate some lower amount for the seller to accept and pay for the remainder, or
3. You could negotiate a sales price that matches the appraised price, or
4. You could cancel the deal and get your earnest money back.

Key Point: This should explain why cash is king. A cash offer is not contingent on lender approval, making it a much safer offer for a seller to accept. For this reason, cash can be worth a five to ten percent discount in some markets and at some price points. It's also why, if you're competing with a cash offer and you're financing, it might be very difficult for you to win.

A cash buyer can be countered to a certain extent if you're willing to state in the contract that you'll cover the gap created by a low appraisal. Think about it. If you weren't willing to make up this difference, it doesn't matter what you offer. You could offer $800,000 in our example because the result is the same: The house doesn't appraise for the amount offered and you're not chipping in to make up the difference. What do you care? You might as well offer a million dollars.

In this scenario, the seller isn't likely to accept some wild, high offer that can't be substantiated by comps. It's a waste of everyone's time. They'll only accept if you, the buyer, are willing to make up the difference between the offer and the appraisal amount. This comes into play in a seller's market all the time.

However, in a buyer's market, it's almost never an issue. In a buyer's market, you probably already paid less than asking because you have the leverage. If the appraisal doesn't come at the agreed-to price, you can go back to the seller and ask them to reduce the price to match the appraisal. "Well, Mrs. Seller, the house only appraised at $450,000 and I can't get a loan for the $500,000 we agreed to, so how do you want to work out the $50,000?"

The seller might agree to reduce the price to match the appraised value. You could also come to terms on splitting the difference because, after all, you want the house. For this reason, you should look at the appraisal as a third negotiating opportunity. But only in a buyer's market. In a seller's market, you've likely already spelled out, inside the terms of the offer, your willingness to handle any low appraisal.

Appraisals are sort of a funny thing. The appraiser's job is to protect the lender's loan. That's it. They provide a subjective value for the house that the lender uses as an objective value. But it's not an objective value. There is no objective value. The house, any house, is only worth what someone will pay for it. You offered X dollars for this house because you decided that's what it's worth to you. The bank is making sure they can resell it for that amount (should you default) and wants a second opinion – but it's still not an objective value.

I bring this up because I've seen people get *anchored* to the appraised value like it's the "truth" and then make all sorts crazy decisions and second guess themselves. Do the work before you write the offer to make sure you a) know what the likely resale value will be and, b) you feel comfortable moving forward at that price. Operating as if the appraised value is the "truth" might be a function of the way you think about monetary value. Many people look for authorities to determine the truth (about lots of things, not just money). Could this be because their view is authorities look like (are *representative* of) someone who knows something they don't? You'll be best deciding for yourself what your next home is worth.

Avoid Being Shortghanged: Shortcuts to Watch For

- *Representativeness/Anchoring*: Because the appraisal is obtained from a bank doesn't make it the truth. It's still a subjective valuation of the house's potential resale amount. Don't get *anchored* to thinking it's the "true" value.

Points to Remember

- As the buyer, you're also responsible for scheduling and paying for the appraisal. The appraisal is in place to protect the lender, confirming how much the lender might expect to get for the property if they had to resell it.
- The lender won't approve a loan for more than the appraised value.
- In a buyer's market, you'll have the opportunity to ask the seller to lower the price to match the appraised amount or otherwise negotiate how the seller might make up the shortfall.
- In a seller's market, you'll likely have to make up the difference.
- In a very competitive market, you might need to waive the piece of your finance contingency that protects you from low appraisal to remain competitive.

Chapter Fourteen:

The Last Steps:
Final Conditions & Signing

"The best way out is always through."

— Robert Frost

Hurrah! The inspection and re-inspection are complete with repairs done. Hooray! The appraisal is done and matches the approved loan amount. Whew. At this point, you're probably about two weeks from the scheduled closing date.

Now it's time to get out the magnifying glass.

Final Conditions

Everything that's been done, and all the accompanying paperwork now goes into "the black box of underwriting." The underwriter is going to get out their magnifying glass and review every single detail.

Once again, this is why I've stressed that you don't want to use one of the big banks as your lender. The underwriters who work for the big banks are typically far removed, both literally and figuratively. They could be located across the country and there's often no way to talk to them. This sort of distance can create issues and slow the process at the worst possible time.

On the other hand, if you use a local lender, the underwriter could be sitting right down the hall in an office in the same building. They're accessible. If something needs to be addressed, it's easy to call them. The loan officer can walk on over and talk to them. *This is not a negligible advantage.*

The underwriter is going to inspect everything you've claimed about your finances, and everything they can find out about the property. The underwriter is the person who ultimately approves your loan. Yes, you were pre-approved, but at this point you need the final stamp of approval from the underwriter.

Your loan officer can be the friendliest, most helpful person you've ever dealt with, but it's the underwriting department that approves your loan. Now is the time they're going to make sure you didn't go out and buy a car since the time of your pre-approval. They need to ensure you don't have any additional monthly payments that will affect your ability to pay your mortgage. They're going to look at your bank statements to be sure everything looks right and there weren't any unexpected cash deposits that made your financial picture look better than it really is. (Since 9/11, undocumented large cash deposits raise big red flags!)

If you've been working with a great Realtor and a great local lender, everything should be fine at this point. Final conditions tend to bite buyers if they failed to listen to the advice of their lender early in the process, or if the lender didn't care enough to spell out all the details and exactly what steps were needed.

I call final conditions a "black box" because at this point, your Realtor, no matter how great they are, is pretty much out of the equation. There's nothing they can do. Up to this point, if you're like most buyers, you'll be close to your Realtor. You're tight; you've created a relationship; you've been through a lot together since you first sat down for your interview and the pre-shopping consultation. You might be used to speaking every day. However, once the appraisal is done, there's little your real estate agent can do until underwriting is complete.

While, as the CEO, you might not lean on the COO (your Realtor) as much now, you really want to stay in touch with your CFO (your lender).

It's critical that you stay in touch with your lender during this time because you want to be sure that they're shepherding your loan through the underwriting process. Again, at the risk of sounding like a tape loop, a big bank's loan officer, or an online lender, won't be as accessible to you as someone who's entire business rides on your referral later. Small, local lenders need to get the deal done on time to stay in business. The big banks and internet lenders do not.

At some point, underwriting will say: "Appraisal's done; the house is good; your finances are solid; your paper work is in order, so we're going to deliver the docs to escrow."

This is the goal: documents released for signing! You'll know this is happening because at least three days before, you'll receive a seller disclosure form that itemizes all the costs associated with the loan. This is part of a Consumer Protection Bureau regulation to ensure that you have all the information needed, that you know exactly what's happening, and that there's no predatory lending occurring.

Signing

Underwriting is done and documents have been delivered to escrow! That brings us to the next part: signing. It's important to keep in mind that signing is not closing; you're not yet getting the keys to the house.

You can expect signing to take place at the escrow office. Escrow has been diligently holding the earnest money you paid for what, by now, might seem like a long, long time.

The escrow office (or attorney) has also collected all of the supplied documents from the seller and put them all together in your file. They've verified that everything matches state laws and will confirm your transaction is good to go.

> **Side Note:** Certain parts of the country don't use escrow officers but use attorneys. In either case, the job is the same.

You can expect to sign about 100 pages of documents while you're there. Your real estate agent might or might not be there as there's nothing for them to do at signing except smile. The escrow officer or attorney will answer any questions you have about what you're signing.

Signing usually occurs two to three days before closing although same day closes are possible, too. It's rare that you'd ever sign at the same time as the seller.

Once both you and the seller have signed the needed documents, they get packaged up and returned to the lender for final approval. Yes, one more approval process, but at this point, you can probably start to chill that champagne.

Between signing and closing, you'll want to have scheduled a final walk through of the house. It may have been a while since you've seen the place and a lot can happen to a property over the course of the closing process. If it's vacant then there might be vandalism to deal with. If it's occupied, it's possible that the house is nowhere near the condition it needs to be in to be turned over. I've seen damage caused be the seller when they were moving out that we wouldn't have seen but for the walk through. If there is damage or the house is somehow unacceptable, you and your agent are going to need to put the brakes on the transaction until whatever it is gets resolved. This is never fun, but if you hired well, your agent should be prepared to get you through this step. Be thankful problems that kill the deal at this stage are rare.

The shortcuts people fall prey to in these final stages are almost always some form of **Confirmation Bias**. Questions *not asked* are usually a function of this shortcut. Buying a new car, for example, wouldn't happen if the client asked their lender if it was a good idea. (It is not a good idea for those of you keeping score at home). The act of not asking their lender comes from their "already knowing" that it's okay. It doesn't occur to them to ask, so they don't.

I know I've warned people to not take on any large purchases, or switch jobs, or accept any large cash gifts, and I've had clients do these things anyway. Why? Because in their mind, what I warned them of didn't register as applicable to them. They already knew better. They're trusting their own intuition while in the midst of the most expensive financial transaction of their life, and this is generally a recipe for problems.

Closing, Recording, and Keys

It's been a long process. Was it was smooth sailing all the way? Or were there some hairy moments and nail biting? Regardless, you're now finally about to get your dream house!

When all the documents signed have been reviewed by the lender, they'll say, "Release the funds." This is like someone saying, "Release the hounds" but the total opposite as instead of running in fear you'll be celebrating in joy!

The funds go to escrow, and escrow "releases the title to record." They literally send the title to the county, so it can be recorded in your name. The property has switched ownership from the seller to you by deed, and it's now recorded in the county. Depending on your location, it should only take a few hours from the time of release until you're recorded. You'll be notified when this occurs.

So now comes everyone's favorite part: keys! By far, the best part of my job.

If the seller negotiated possession after closing (for example, they need a little extra time to move out), you are still entitled to get keys as you are now the official owner of this house. The loan has been funded, it's been released to record, recorded, and it is now your house.

Congratulations! Pop that cork.

Avoid Being Shortchanged: Shortcuts to Watch For

- *Confirmation Bias:* As you are nearing the end of the process, you might begin to believe you already know what's best at this point. Beware! Despite my warnings and advice, I've seen clients succumb to this heuristic and create huge problems. Stay vigilant and ask before making any major life changes.

Points to Remember

- The paperwork goes into the "black box" of underwriting to let the underwriter review everything with a fine-toothed comb. The underwriter is the person who ultimately approves your loan.
- It's in your best interest to use a local lender because the underwriter is likely to be working locally rather than across the country. Having them accessible to your lender could be the difference between closing on time and not closing at all.
- The underwriter will verify that everything you said about your financial situation, and everything said about the property, are all accurate.
- Your real estate agent can't do much during the underwriting process, and it's a good idea for you to stay in touch with your lender during this time.

- With underwriter approval, documents will be released for signing.
- Don't confuse "signing" with closing. The escrow office will verify that all documents meet state laws, and both you and the seller will have a signing appointment.
- With final lender approval after signing, the funds are released to escrow for closing.
- The property title is released to transfer by deed and recorded in the county office.
- You now own the home and your real estate agent will deliver the keys to you.

Section 3:

Selling

Chapter Fifteen:

Should I Stay or Should I Go?

"The early bird gets the worm, but the second mouse gets the cheese."

– Willie Nelson

"Is this the best time to sell?" "Maybe we should rent our place instead of selling." "Should I be buying my next home, or should I rent for a while?" "What if we just refinance and remodel instead?"

These are the types of questions people often ask me before putting their home on the market. Sometimes the decision is simpler – some circumstances demand a quick and immediate sale – job transfer, family changes, etc. But in many cases, the sale of a home is one of choice; one in which there are many possible, difficult-to-predict, outcomes... just the type of scenario in which the human brain relies heavily on shortcuts and would be better served by a more rational approach.

To avoid the common shortcuts normally used in seeking the answers, let's break the question of whether to sell now, or not, into two categories:

1. What does the money say to do?
2. What creates the highest quality of life?

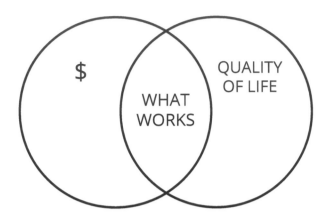

Cue Venn diagram music (I'm a sucker for Venn diagrams)
In the money circle you'd put things like:
- How much could you sell your home for?
- How much could you rent it for?
- What are the associated costs with either?
- What would it cost to buy where you're moving?
- What would it cost to rent?
- Do you need to sell before you buy?
- How much would it cost to remodel your current home?

You'd fill the quality of life circle with questions like:
- What would it be like for each kid to have their own room?
- Or, what would it be like to no longer have to maintain a home big enough for kids who are gone?
- What are the public schools like near my current, and proposed, home?
- What is the commute like from either location?
- Are their crime issues?
- Do I want to be closer or farther from the city?

But don't commute times have a dollar cost to them? The difference between public and private school certainly does. Renting has a quality of life cost as well as a monetary cost. Mess around with this Venn diagram long enough, and you'll notice something: Questions that at first blush fit neatly on the money side can shift into the quality of life side. Quality of life issues likewise almost always come with a monetary cost.

Buying a home is not always better than renting. Owning a home you rent to others to build equity is not the best path to wealth for everyone. These are individual choices, not something decreed from on high. That we're, by default, looking for the "right" answer (not only in matters of real estate) is often invisible to us.

We live as if there are choices that are inherently right or wrong and then demand we find the "right" one. Little creates more stress, and less joy, than pretending we could make the wrong choice.

Have you considered that, maybe, the only "right" answer is the one you can own as the right answer for you right now – at this very moment?

Considering the thought process will give you some power with the choice you make.

> **Key Point:** There are no "right" answers, only answers that are "right" now.

When you see that *Confirmation Bias* skews the very act of looking, you're not tied as tightly to the answers your looking provides. Notice how unexamined, pre-existing notions color the process. What do you already know to be true about the situation? What are you certain about? These are usually flags to where *Confirmation Bias* lay in hiding.

Watch for how, once you find "the answers," you stop looking for alternate possibilities. Can you catch yourself collecting evidence that the choice you made was that holy grail of all choices, the "*right choice*"?

The ***Availability Heuristic*** will likely have you put a disproportionate amount of weight on what passes for "news." Interest Rates Are Going UP! Housing Prices Reach New Highs! It's hard to escape these headlines at every turn.

Unfortunately, what isn't as readily ***available*** is that this "news" (like all news) is generated to sell advertising. Prices, like interest rates, go up and down. Uh, excuse me, but that's not news. What's new about that? Think about it. It can only be "news" the first time you hear about it. The rest of the time it's more likely to be hype than relevant.

Is the latest "peak" the top? Neither you nor the talking head have any way of knowing. Are increasing interest rates going to mean a rush of buyers or an end to the rush of buyers? Anyone pretending to know the answer is doing just that. Pretending.

Consider, if you practice being present, you cannot make the wrong choice. It's not that it doesn't matter what you choose. It matters. There will be consequences either way. But because it matters is not to say there's a right and a wrong choice. If you honestly looked for an answer, and you can be responsible for your choice, then that's the right answer.

To illustrate the malleable nature of this type of choice, let's look at a friend of mine. This is a woman who is brilliant in many ways, and is a very successful wealth manager and financial consultant. She lives in Silicon Valley, one of the hottest real estate markets in the country. This woman has a mastery of the costs and benefits of long-term renting vs. home ownership in a way that, when I think about it, makes my eyes roll back in my head. Up until recently, she's been clear that, with what she's committed to in life and what's important to her, renting her home and not owning made the most sense.

Then two things changed. First, her family became 50 percent larger when she and her husband welcomed their baby daughter into the world. Second, her landlord called and told her he was going to take advantage of the hot market and sell. They had 60 days to vamoose!

Now, either of those things happening on their own might not have been enough to shift her personal Venn diagram. But both of these changing at the same time, and the overlap, the "what works" intersection, changed in a moment. I've never seen anybody, in any market, pull it together so quickly and manifest the perfect home to buy.

Did any of the fundamental financial considerations that make owning a home vs. renting change? Not really. It's not "a great time to buy." In fact, she could be very well could be buying at the very peak of the next bubble. She was happy with the financial implications of being a renter when she had a baby, and moving from time to time when it was just her and her hubby was an acceptable lifestyle. But change both those items at the same time and the "what works" for her changed. There was now a new set of concerns. The items in her circles received new weighting. A new answer into the "what works" section appeared.

Again, my point: There are no "right" answers, only answers that are "right" now.

This is true of most, if not all, complex choices with uncertain outcomes we face in life. Instead of looking for certainty in the answers, we'd be better served by looking for certainty in the process by which we come up with the answers. Keep an eye out for potential shortcuts, watch for anyone, including ourselves, claiming a direct line to the "truth."

Did my friend make the "right" choice? How could anyone from the outside say? Could she have continued to rent and called it the "right" choice? Of course. But because her thinking is clear, no matter what happens next, in the market or in her life, she'll make her next brilliant decision and move on from there.

Is it the right time to sell? Who are you asking? Do the work. Investigate everything. Keep looking. Ask questions. Don't chase the market. Stay informed. Be willing to trust yourself to find the "right now" answer for you. And if it is the time to sell, for you, the chapters that follow will help guide you to the best possible outcome.

Avoid Being Shortchanged: Shortcuts to Watch For

- *Confirmation Bias*: You might be only considering the information that already supports what you believe to be true both about the value of your home and the best time to sell.
- *Availability Heuristic*: Constant bombardment of news of the booming market and of historically low interest rates that will rise can place an undue weight on your decision to sell now.
- *Prospect Theory and loss avoidance:* These could pull to keep you from acting. Weigh all the factors, money and quality of life, and move forward.

Points to Remember

- Only you can ultimately determine when it's the right time to sell.
- Stop pretending there is a "right" answer out there, or that you could make the "wrong" choice.
- Interest rates and home prices go up and down. That's not news.
- Nobody can predict the future.
- Don't be pressured. Sell only when you are ready.
- Your circumstances are unique and constantly changing. Doing the work to make a rational decision will leave you able to trust yourself.

Chapter Sixteen:

Who's the Boss?

"The best executive is the one who has sense enough to pick good men to do what he wants done, and self-restraint to keep from meddling with them while they do it."

– Theodore Roosevelt

Okay – so it's time to sell. You've made the call and you're ready. Let's get started.

As discussed in Chapter 3, I'm proceeding under the assumption that you've created the mindset for selling your home that's something like: "You're the CEO of company that's in the business of selling a commodity in an established marketplace for the most money, in the least time, with the least hassle."

This mindset does two things. First, being the CEO will allow you to ask questions! You're now the person who owns the desk upon which the buck stops. It's your business. See something you don't know about? Great, it's your company. Ask about it. Check it out. Make sure you understand it.

The second thing this mindset does is create the specific kind of business you are in. Most sellers, and many real estate agents for that matter, miss this completely. While the CEO part might be simple to understand, notice the other operative words in this context: commodity and marketplace.

I find that this is a new concept to most sellers and very likely, for you as well. I rarely find a seller who approaches the transaction using this paradigm. Instead, most people approach selling their home as just that: "I'm selling my home."

This is problematic on a few levels. To start with, and to be very blunt, no one wants to buy *your home*!

Of course, I understand that it's your home. It's near and dear to your heart because of the memories you made there. It could be your first home as a newlywed or the home in which you raised your children. It was a place in which you spent a lot of blood, sweat, and possibly tears on its upkeep and maintenance. You marked the kids' growth lines on the door frame. The backyard contains the flowers and plants you've added over the years. Yes, it's definitely your home.

And yet, let me repeat: No one wants to buy "your home." They want to buy a house and then turn it into their home. Think about when you purchased the property, however long ago that may have been. It wasn't "your home" when you made the offer and bought it. It was a house – a property within your budget and in the location or with the amenities you wanted. After you took possession of the keys, you turned it in your home. How long did that transformation take? Three months? Six months? A year? More? Do you remember when it started to feel like your home?

The bottom line is: nobody is looking to buy "your home," and here's where you have to be very aware of the *Endowment Effect*. You're likely to overvalue what you consider to be near and dear to you, only because it's near and dear to you.

If you price and market your home from anything less than "it's a commodity in a marketplace of similar commodities," you're in for the same battle that kills thousands of businesses every day. Businesses that focus on, and value, their product or service more than the market end up out of business.

Buyers care little about most of the improvements you've made to the property and care less about the memories you made there. Of course, some of the same amenities that you love are attracting them, but still, they're not buying "your home." The people who make up the marketplace are looking for a "house" to make into their own home.

Get Ready to Compete

As the CEO, you need to be cognizant of, and responsible for, what the market is looking for and what it sees when it looks at what you're selling. You're selling something that other people are also selling and that makes it a commodity. No matter how low the housing inventory may be when you're selling, there are still other people who are selling the same thing you are.

You must get used to this idea. You are competing in a marketplace. There will be other houses for sale at a comparable price, and there's going to be a competition. You're competing for buyers, and while the house you're selling may be nicer than others, others may be nicer than yours. Some people will be priced a little higher, some a little lower. You're even competing against similarly priced rentals, and what it costs to refinance and remodel – all options for the people you're looking to attract. Picture an open-air market with vendors of all kinds hawking their wares. That's you in the marketplace. Let the games begin!

Granted, if you're in a hot seller's market, you might not have to compete very hard for buyers. Buyers will be competing hard with each other for your property since there's less inventory. On the other hand, when it's a buyer's market, you're going to have to compete very, very hard. But no matter the market conditions, top dollar goes to the house that most fits the needs of the most number of buyers. (Again, this is a principle not limited to real estate.)

It's a business, and you're in charge. You must start thinking like any CEO running a business. You need to approach this process with a definitive plan to attract the right buyer and have that buyer pay enough to cover your expenses and the hassle of selling your house, or your business won't make any money. That's how business works! Businesses are in business to turn a profit by selling whatever product or service they offer. You must adjust your own mindset to think in those terms.

That idea – selling – may make you very uncomfortable. Some people get queasy at the thought of selling and know they're not suited for the task. Fair enough. If you fall into that category, you'll need to hire a sales person. This doesn't have to be you, the CEO. That's a big piece of why people hire Realtors – to act as the sales person.

At the risk of beating the same dead parrot we killed earlier, be clear: *You're* the CEO in this business, and no good CEO would ever hire a sales person without interviewing them to ensure they're the right fit for the job. More than 70 percent of all sellers hire the first agent they talk to. That's a wacky way to run a company, don't you think?

A good CEO would want to see the track record of any potential hire, wouldn't they? Sure, the interviewee may say all the right things, but their recent sales record is where proverbial rubber meets the road.

Do not let yourself fall victim to the **Representativeness** or **Availability Heuristics**. Nothing trumps a track record. Does the person dress like a Realtor? That's nice. Have you seen a lot of their signs in the neighborhood? Oh, that's cool. Seen their ads in the paper? Great. But what about the last 12 months of sales? How many have they done? What is their sold-to-list price ratio? How many days on market do they average? And how do those numbers compare to the base line average in your market?

Your business has a specific goal. To sell your home for the most money, in the least time, with the least hassle. If you are hiring someone to help, shouldn't they have a track record that shows they've done that before? We've covered the tough questions in an earlier chapter, and as the CEO, you'll have to ask some tough questions. Go back and review those questions if you need to.

Good CEOs don't make hires based on appearances or because of some tenuous, sort of off-handed referral – the ol' cousin's wife's best friend's husband sort of recommendation. If you don't act as the CEO, either by mistake or by choice, you'll end up with a business that takes whatever it gets. What you won't get is the best price in the least amount of time and with the least hassle for the house you're selling!

An exceedingly common pitfall people make, almost entirely due to *Availability*, is thinking that they need to hire someone who "specializes" in their neighborhood. As I pointed out earlier, this is lazy thinking as there is no real logic to it. What special knowledge do you think a "neighborhood specialist" has? What value do they provide to the buyer (your customer)?

When you went to buy your home, did you give a second thought to what the agent representing the seller knew about the neighborhood? Buyers might want a neighborhood specialist to represent them, but as a seller, there's rarely value they add over their track record of getting the most money in the least time.

In fact, if you dig deeper into the thinking, wouldn't you want the person representing you to be skilled enough that no matter where they sold homes, they were reliable at getting more for the homes they sell than local averages? That's the skill set you, as the CEO, should be looking for in your COO/CMO.

Deeper still lies the way in which the agent became to be thought of as a "neighborhood expert" and why you think that hiring a neighborhood expert is important in the first place. Realtors are not stupid – they know that people buy based on

Availability – that consumers are all likely to go with the name that comes most easily to their mind. For this reason they've created a practice called "farming." As we previously covered, farming is when an agent picks a neighborhood they'd like to work and then expends the effort to be the person people in that area think of first. They send postcards, run open houses, knock on doors, create neighborhood events, and as they begin to list and sell houses in that area, they get to put their signs in the yards of all the neighbors. Pretty soon, when anyone in that area thinks of an agent, their name comes to mind first.

This means if you are thinking of hiring a neighborhood expert because you've seen their name a lot, just keep in mind, it's likely you're turning yourself into someone else's crop. You've been farmed.

I am not saying that's the wrong person to hire; I'm saying that I can think of few examples of the special "value" they can add simply because they chose your area as their farm. There are exceptions, like if you are selling a condo with an especially tricky HOA, but these are far less common than people think.

I'd get more interested in who knows how to attract and negotiate with those customers, aka buyers. Hiring someone who has a track record of selling homes, regardless of neighborhood, for more money in the least time is more likely to produce the results you want than someone who chose to "farm" you.

As the boss, your job is to hire the person who will bring the most value to the table – both for you, and your customer. Choose wisely.

Avoid Being Shortchanged: Shortcuts to Watch For

- *Endowment Effect*: You're not selling "your home." You are selling a house. No one wants to buy "your home," so you must disconnect from this idea and be cautious of over valuing it, simply because it's yours.

154

- *Representativeness:* When it comes to selecting a Realtor, choosing an agent who fits your preconceived idea of what they should look like vs. carefully inspecting their track record is a mistake.
- *Availability*: Realtors farm neighborhoods specifically to become top of mind, to become *available* to you, when you think of an agent. There is rarely any secret value a "neighborhood expert" selling a home can add to the equation.

Points to Remember

- Your goal in selling: Get the most money in the least amount of time with the least hassle. It's that simple.
- Change your perspective. The paradigm you're looking for is you're the CEO of a company that is selling a commodity in an existing marketplace.
- You are not selling "your home" because no one wants to buy "your home." They want to buy "their home."
- Your house is a commodity, even in a tight market. There will be others selling and you have to compete.
- If selling makes you uncomfortable, hire a sales person to represent you – a Realtor.
- No CEO of a company would hire someone without interviewing that person and knowing what their track record is.

Chapter Seventeen:

Home Valuation or...
Nobody Cares What You Think

"Reality doesn't care if you believe it."

– Bobba Fett

Quick. Make a list of all the factors that determine whether your house sells, and how long it'll take. What would you put on there?

Price?

Size?

Market condition?

Strength of the local economy?

Age?

Proximity to amenities?

Quality of neighborhood schools?

What's interesting about this exercise is there's at least one thing you'd never add (and I don't care how long I gave you to make the list):

Your personal opinions.

Why I say this is interesting is because, while nobody would add their personal assessment of value to a list of factors that determine the price the market will pay, they often operate as if their opinion matters.

It doesn't.

It's not uncommon for people to operate as if the price the market will offer them is somehow magically determined by what they think.

It isn't.

Not even a little.

Have you ever watched the TV show, *Shark Tank*? It's a reality game show in which entrepreneurs come on and pitch five very successful business people and investors (the "Sharks") in hopes of getting an investment in their company. I'd guess somewhere close to half of these contestants put valuations on their companies that are quite literally laughable. I mean the "Sharks" actually laugh at them, on TV, for thinking their company is worth more than the evidence proves or even suggests. Those people, when unwilling to reevaluate the value they first placed on their company, leave the show empty handed.

In selling your house, as the CEO of a company selling a commodity, you must approach the market, not from what you think your home is worth, but from what the market has said it will pay for similar versions of the commodity you're selling. When selling a house, the number one determining factor in whether the house sells, and the length of time it takes to sell it, is price. Sure, the marketing matters as does the presentation and a host of other issues, but these all pale next to the difference price makes.

Price your house correctly and you'll compensate for most other flaws. Price it incorrectly, and nothing else you do matters. Price is king. End. Of. Story.

Have I mentioned you're selling a commodity? Well, I keep saying it because it's important. No matter how great you think your house and property are, it remains a commodity. And regardless of the commodity – it could be marbles, ponies, paper clips, or cars – when people have some other version to spend their money on, price is king.

Rare is the marketing that will sell two nickels for a quarter. If the corner grocery sells milk for $5.00/gallon and you own a store across the street trying to sell the same milk for $8.00/gallon, you're going to have a problem. You could dump money into advertising, but in the end, you'll likely only let more people know your milk is overpriced.

Sure, Starbucks has created something that allows them to sell a cup of coffee for $8.00. They found a way to turn a commodity (coffee) into a unique and desirable experience. Can you do that for your house? Maybe. But no matter how much money you might have to experiment, there's at least one major difference: You only have one shot at this. It's not a test and adapt system for you. You have one house, and in almost all cases, you'll have just one shot to get it right.

As the CEO, you want to watch how the market behaves when shopping for the commodity you're selling. When the market shops for houses, it does so by beginning its search at certain price points. Price is the primary driver of the home buyer (your potential customer). Even when there's not a lot of competition and you're in a seller's market, price is still king, by virtue of how the market shops for your commodity. The number of people shopping for homes right now, thinking, "I want a home in your neighborhood and money is no object" can probably be counted on one hand by a 2-year-old who can't count yet.

You need to figure out from the buyer's perspective how much someone would be willing to spend for a house like yours. Remember, you're not selling your home; you're selling a house, and there's big difference! (If you are still struggling with this concept, please reread the previous chapter.)

Start with determining that given the age, size, amenities, condition, acreage, and location, what your house is likely to be worth in the current marketplace. The good news is that there are a few ways to go about placing a value on your house, and one way not to do it.

No matter what method you use to value your house, do not use the Zestimate (Zillow's price estimator) or other similar online calculators. The Zestimate is dangerous. As I said earlier, by their own admission, which you can read on their website, the median error for the Zestimate is five percent! This means half the homes are off by *more* than five percent and half are off by less. Which half your home falls into can be determined by flipping a coin. Good luck with that.

We discussed this shortcut in the buying section. The Zestimate will create an *anchor*. You'll have no choice but to use that number in your mental assessment. Thanks to the Zestimate, you'll have a supposed value locked in your brain that is likely off by more than the value of a new Mercedes. You might as well throw a dart at a wall of prices and use that. Add to the mix that, if the number is agreeable to you, *Confirmation Bias* will jump in and you'll be even more likely to price your house poorly.

Even before looking at Zillow, I'll venture that you already had an inflated value in mind. Why would I think that? The *Endowment Effect.* You own it, so you're predisposed to thinking it's more valuable than the market will.

Most people start with an inflated number, then the Zestimate *anchors* it in their mind, and the natural psychological tendency for *Confirmation Bias* seals the deal. Ouch. I almost feel sorry for your agent. The Zestimate is not the way to go about valuing your house, and again, I strongly suggest you don't even look at it.

Better Ways to Value Your House

First, visit open houses in your neighborhood before you ever put your house on the market. By "your neighborhood," that could mean within about a one- to two-mile radius of where you live or it could mean within your development. I trust you'll have a sense of your own neighborhood when it comes to an apples-to-apples comparison of your house against others. Do you live in a more upscale development than the surrounding area? Your house — with its age, size, amenities, etc. – will sell for more than house in a different development. That's easy to accept.

Conversely, maybe within that a few blocks is a newer development or subdivision with recently constructed homes that have all the latest amenities – granite counter tops, hardwood floors, etc. Obviously, these will sell for more than your 50s-era ranch despite their physical proximity to each other. If you can start going to these open houses two to three months before putting your own house on the market, do so. Spend the time in your area and determine what houses are selling for, or at least what their asking prices are.

With enough lead time, you'll also be able to determine what houses sold for. Remember – asking price and sold price are different things. Just because your neighbor is asking $550,000 for their house doesn't mean that's what it's worth. It's only worth what someone paid for it and you'll need to research that (or ask them). Sold prices are part of public records but aren't recorded until after the sale in finalized, usually about 30 days from the time an offer is accepted. So, if your neighbor went under contract with their house last week, you can't be certain what it sold for, unless they tell you, for about a month.

With this information, you can start building a record that includes asking prices, sold prices (if you can uncover that), and calculations of price per square foot. For the best comparison, you will want to pay attention to those properties that are in about 300- to 400-square-feet of the size of your house, either larger or smaller. It's not exact, but it's a good rule of thumb to use.

You can also compare the number of bedrooms and you can use houses that have +/– 1 compared to yours. For example, if you have a three-bedroom house, you could use a four-bedroom house as a comparison, but I wouldn't use one with five bedrooms. The number of bathrooms also creates a good comparative metric, keeping in mind bathrooms are worth more than bedrooms. In other words, a house with the same square footage that has three bedrooms versus one with four bedrooms won't vary in value as much as one with two baths will compared to a similar one-bath house. This makes sense, because it's far more expensive and complicated to put in a bathroom than it is to turn empty space into a bedroom.

You'll begin to get a sense of how the contributing factors impact price as you do this. Yes, it takes time and effort, but as the CEO, shouldn't you put in the time and effort so that you get a solid education about the marketplace in which you're selling?

Of course, as the CEO, you could hire someone who has this kind of useful market information. I believe those people are called Realtors. But of course, if you don't do this work yourself and you hire someone for their market knowledge, you really do give up the right to second guess them (and you might have been looking forward to that).

To get a market expert's opinion, I'd call two or three Realtors and ask for a comparative market analysis (CMA). Any agent should do this for you. I've heard of agents who charge for these, and in my view, that's a fantastic way for them to advertise that they're horrible agents. Always nice to find out before you talk to them. Realtors who want your business should be happy to provide you with a CMA.

Remember, you're the CEO. Asking for a CMA is like asking for a quote from any service provider. You're offering a valuable commodity to a real estate agent – a commission on the sale price of your house. It's a lot of money. Don't hesitate to ask for what you need.

Key Point: A good Realtor should be happy to help you place an accurate value on your property.

When I provide a CMA to people who ask me for one, I give them a 25- to 30-page report with hand-written notes with my own input and perspective. It's part of my own marketing and prospecting. Asking for a CMA could be the start of the interview process you use before selecting the Realtor with whom you're going to work to sell your house.

When reading the CMA, what you want to look for is the evidence that suggests what people will pay for your home. Many people look for the agent "who says they can sell my home for the most." That's a silly game. Asking price and sold price are two different things. Anyone can promise to sell your home for any dollar amount you want to hear. You need to look at the *evidence the marketplace is providing* and decide for yourself.

As a CEO selling a commodity in a marketplace, look at the evidence and ask yourself, "If I were a buyer today, seeing what else I could spend my money on, how much would I pay for my house?" Thinking like a buyer is standard operating procedure when bringing a product to market, yet it's shocking how few home sellers take the time to do it thoroughly.

Whether you go to open houses, search online, or use the CMAs that your potential real estate agents provide to you, you'll now have a reasonable picture of the value of your house.

> **Key Point:** Notice how in none of this work what you thought your house was worth became an issue. That's because the market doesn't care what you think. If you remember nothing else, remember: *You are doing this work not to set the price you want but to see if the price the market is offering is a price you'd accept.* There's no shame in not selling because the market won't pay what you need, but it's silly to think the market is going to offer you more because you think it should.

Avoid Being Shortchanged: Shortcuts to Watch For

- *Anchoring Heuristic*: If you make the mistake of using the Zestimate to gauge the value of your house, you'll likely fall victim to *Anchoring* and will face frustration when the actual value is revealed as lower than that which is serving as an *anchor* to you.
- *Endowment Effect*: Since you own your house, you already believe that it's worth more than others do.
- *Confirmation Bias*: You start with an inflated number in your head, and then the Zestimate confirms it. This will make learning the actual value – the one the marketplace will truly bear out – difficult, if not impossible.

Points to Remember

- No matter how you slice it, price is king (and price will always be king) when trying to sell your house.
- Avoid Zillow and the Zestimate (and any similar online calculator) completely. You will not get an accurate number and the *Anchor* effect will skew your thinking.
- In the two to three months before you list, visit open houses in your area that are comparable to your house. Keep track of asking prices, sales prices (if you can find them), and calculate price per square foot. This is the best way to educate yourself about the marketplace you're in.
- Alternatively, ask two or three agents for a comparative market analysis (CMA) as part of your interview process. They should be happy to supply it.
- The market – in this case, potential buyers – set the price. You don't.

Chapter Eighteen:

Preparation – Ready, Steady, Go

"The separation is in the preparation."

– Russell Wilson

Okay. You've got a close enough approximation for what the market will pay for a house like yours and it's a price you are willing to accept. Good work. Now, it's time to maximize every opportunity for getting the highest possible price. Let's talk about what there is to do, and what there is to watch for, as you prep your home for the market.

First, look for some of the shortcuts we've already discussed. Remember: the market is looking to buy a house, not your home. This is the most important part of preparing your house. You'll need to make it look like it could become someone else's home.

There are tons of articles and content that you can find online about staging your house for sale, and a lot of it's very valuable, but unless you can come to terms with the fact that you're not selling *your home* – you can only sell *a house* – you're going to struggle to get the most money in the least amount of time.

Your family photos, the knick knacks, the tchotchkes all around your house make it your home, while simultaneously, preventing it from looking like it could be someone else's. This is an immediate turn off to buyers. Buyers want to see blank walls and generally open space. They want to be able to envision their "stuff" in the house. The more of your stuff they see, the less able they are to see their own stuff in place of it.

If you can't get rid of your "stuff" before you go to market, work with a good home stager and/or downsizing company. You're already struggling with the *Endowment Effect* and you think your stuff is valuable, so gaining the perspective of a professional and neutral, third party is a wise investment. Many Realtors have referrals in this regard, and if you're already using a professional to help sell your home, go with their people.

Stagers are experts at getting rid of clutter, have a better eye for positioning furniture in the most effective way, can repurpose your "junk" room into usable space, understand the impact of lighting and how to make spaces look larger creating a neutral yet inviting space. Stagers understand what buyers are looking for and can help you achieve that in your house.

Buyers are notorious for making snap decisions, and yes, first impressions matter a great deal. They'll pull up to the curb and immediately notice if the flower beds are weeded, if it's clean or dirty, and if the paint is in good shape. With that in mind, you want the curb appeal to pop and for the house to be spotless. As with staging, it often pays to hand off this preparation to professional cleaners and landscapers.

Watch out for the impact of *Prospect Theory*. Remember, as humans, we're more concerned about, and will risk more, to avoid loss than we will to gain. A cash outlay to pay for professional cleaning and landscapers to spruce up your house is an expense, and in your mind, could represent a loss. I assure you, you'll get a solid return on this investment. Watch for pennywise, pound foolish shortcuts here.

Key Point: Placing your house for sale is the worst time to get cheap about paying a professional.

Beyond Cleaning and Weeding

I've never been clear as to why this occurs, but people who balk at spending $500 to have their house deep cleaned and polished are often the same people who say they are putting off selling until they remodel the kitchen. Maybe I should write a book on people's irrational relationship to selling their homes. Hmmmm...

Nevertheless, I get countless clients who tell me they're going to list the house after they remodel the kitchen or update a bathroom. What about the basement? If we turn that into a rec room, that'll add value, right?

Wrong.

I've almost never seen an extensive renovation return a positive ROI when done immediately prior to sale. At best, people get 90 cents back for every dollar they spend.

Exceptions are generally only in updates that are structural in nature (e.g., repairing a roof, fixing a leak in the basement, etc.). For items that a potential buyer might demand a repair prior to closing, then it is worth considering, but mostly the standard remodeling people talk about won't generate more at the sale than you paid to have it done.

Additionally, remodeling tends to ignore the timeline you initially create. In fact, remodels seem to go on forever. Once you start, you'll likely uncover something else that needs to be done. It turns into a creep project really fast. It's like the guy who decided to replace the cracked switch plate and ended up repainting the living room, only to then replace the carpet, and ultimately buy new furniture – all for a $1.79 switch plate.

You only remodel a house that you intend to continue living in, so you can enjoy the improved space and amenities. Then when you decide to sell, you'll get the same 75 to 90 percent of the value of your investment back but will have gotten to enjoy the upgrades yourself.

Cosmetic work worth doing is patching and painting, but not much else. Paint adds to the "clean, fresh" feel the market is looking for. If you do decide to paint, choose a very neutral color! Why? The corollary to the rule of "nobody cares what you think" is "nobody likes your taste either." Off-white (and there are plenty of shades that fall into this category) is always an excellent choice.

Home Inspection

Now that remodeling is off the table, let's go deeper into repairs and some of the implications of those. I recommend that you go ahead and pay for a home inspection – before you put the house on the market.

"What? Huh? Home inspection? Isn't that in the Buying section of the book?"

Yes, buyers are usually prepared to pay for a home inspection, but as the seller, you stand to save thousands of dollars by doing one yourself. Spend a little to save a lot! (See: **Prospect Theory** if you want to know why you might resist this.)

First, the inspection will point out any flaws and damage that the buyer is going to discover anyway, so it puts you ahead of that train. People sometimes express the concern that if the inspector uncovers some previously unknown defect they, as the seller, will now need to disclose that. Yes. This is true. You will need to disclose anything you discover. But, if you discover it through the inspection, so will they. There's nothing you'll find out about the house as a result of the inspection that the buyer won't learn later.

The benefit is that you will learn it first. If you wait for the buyer to do an inspection, especially if it's post-offer, your home will be off the market when they start asking for repairs. That entire renegotiation takes place when you have almost no leverage. You're losing time, and if you decline to make the repairs, your option is to go back on the market while explaining to every other buyer the conditions that were uncovered and you're unwilling to fix. Does that sound like a place from which you'll get the most money in the least time?

The buyer is in a premium negotiating position to nickel and dime you over the inspection report. There is nothing to stop them from asking for a $10,000 price reduction for something that would've cost you $5,000 to repair.

If the inspection report does turn up a $5,000 repair, for example, you can go ahead and take care of that before the house goes on the market. You can also share the report with potential buyers, with complete transparency of the true condition of the house. You'll be showing what you've repaired, and more importantly, what you won't be repairing. Their offer is now going to be based on the actual condition of the house. No nickel and diming later.

This is the most important aspect of doing the inspection before listing. The potential to cut out what amounts to a second round of negotiations (see Chapter 12 on home inspections in the Buying section) cannot be overstated. You've shared the inspection report and based the asking price on its findings. The buyer knows what they're getting, and, more times than not, this will eliminate any secondary negotiations once you've mutually agreed to terms.

Is this a radical approach? I don't know. It'll cost you about $500 for an inspection. That'll be an added "expense." But anything you pay to repair, as a result of the inspection, you were likely going to have to spend anyway – either in repair cost or reduced price. Doing it before the sale saves you from getting hit with it after you're under contract and have lost your leverage..

Don't obsess about uncovering something disastrous or losing $500. If something major is uncovered, you'll have saved thousands by finding out now, before incurring the other expenses of going to market.

In a buyer's market or a down-trending seller's market, having an inspection will often generate more offers because you've removed one barrier to entry for buyers. The easier you can make it for buyers to make an offer on your house, the more offers you're likely to get. More offers mean more demand and when increased demand meets limited supply, one thing happens. Price rises.

As the CEO of a company out to sell a commodity, your having completed a pre-inspection also has the advantage of setting you apart in the market place. Suppose a buyer has a choice of two houses:

- Your house, where they are handed a full inspection report, along with the receipts and warranties of any recent repairs. The buyer is clear about what they are getting and what they are paying for.
- Some other house, which while otherwise similar, has no inspection report. The buyer is not clear what surprises the inspection will turn up, or if after finding out, the seller is in a position to correct any defects.

Which is more appealing to the buyer? You might even consider the impact **Prospect Theory** might have on the buyers. Which of the two represents a greater risk of loss to the buyer?

In my view, a pre-inspection is the best $500 you can spend as a seller in a real estate transaction and handling this appropriately will complete the physical preparation for sale.

Avoid Being Shortchanged: Shortcuts to Watch For

- **Prospect Theory:** Don't think of paying for cleaning, staging, inspections and repairs as losses. They represent investments that will produce gains in the end.
- **Prospect Theory:** Plays for a buyer, too. Presenting a complete inspection report could alleviate their fear of loss.

- ***Endowment Effect***: Your view of what to keep and what to get rid of before putting your house on the market could be skewed. Your taste is not everyone's taste. Get a professional opinion about how to prepare.

Points to Remember

- You are selling a house, not your home. Get rid of personal photos and knick knacks around the house. They're a turn off to buyers.
- Consider working with a home stager. They understand what buyers are looking for and can prepare your house accordingly.
- Buyers make snap decisions and first impressions rule, so your house must be sparkling clean both inside and out. Consider professional cleaning and landscaping services.
- There is rarely a point to doing any remodeling in order to put your house on the market. You'll almost never recoup your investment!
- A home inspection will indicate anything that needs attention or repair. Paying for an inspection as the seller can put you in front of the train and ultimately pays off by potentially eliminating a second round of negotiations.

Chapter Nineteen:

Look at me! Look at me!

"Doing business without advertising is like winking at a girl in the dark. You know what you are doing, but nobody else does."
– SH Britt

Once you're confident about the price you're going to ask for your house, and you've had it inspected, repaired, cleaned, staged and polished, you're ready to tell the market all about your place. It's time to promote your commodity to the world. Promotion generally falls into one of two categories: marketing and prospecting.

> **Key Point:** Since you're looking for the most money in the least time, you'll need to do both marketing and prospecting. The amount you get for your house is, in a large part, determined by both the *quantity* of people who *find your house* and the *quality* of what they *find out about your house*.

Marketing Your House

The marketing aspect includes placing it on the Multiple Listing Service (MLS), which in turn will have it show up on the major public-facing websites like Zillow, Redfin, and the rest of the gang.

It also includes putting up fliers, placing a sign in the yard, and online advertising on social media sites like Facebook. I recommend that you do all these things. For the reasons I explain below, I won't be bothering with a deep dive into various marketing strategies. I will, however, point out some mental shortcuts and otherwise overlooked aspects about promoting your house.

If you've already hired a real estate agent to handle the sale for you – and you hired them based on their *track record of selling homes for more money in less time* – they'll have their own successful marketing approach and will handle all of this for you.

How can you be sure their marketing approach and strategy are successful? You've already uncovered that based on their track record! If they sell homes for more money in less time, whatever they do is working. Steve Jobs used to say he hired brilliant people and then let them work. He was pretty good at that whole CEO thing. You might want to take his advice.

As mentioned earlier, one of the most useless comparisons you can attempt to make, as a way of determining if a given agent is more likely to sell your house, is to compare marketing strategies. How would you know a good plan or strategy one from a bad one? It's pure **Representativeness** at play. You're going to prefer the one that most mimics the idea you have in mind of a successful marketing campaign. Without seeing their track record of sales, compared to local averages, it's meaningless, and after seeing their track record, it's sort of pointless.

I don't care how much you think their being "familiar" with your neighborhood is important, or how much you love the idea that they have a kiosk at a local mall. If they underperform, then those are things the market doesn't care about. It's that simple.

That said, there are a few things to know about marketing a property, especially if you are going it alone. (BTW: If you go it alone, then interviewing top agents and asking about their marketing strategies so you can copy them is brilliant, and since all good agents have a servant's heart, they should be happy to share with you anything you might want to know. I'm not being facetious – good agents are in business to build relationships and are happy to share their ideas.)

The most obvious place to market your home is your local Multiple Listing Service (known as the MLS). Every major market has some version of one. It's a collection of all available homes for sale by the real estate agents of a given geographic region. It's from this collection of listings that Zillow, Redfin, Realtor.com, and the like, get the homes they show to consumers.

Do I have to explain the significance of having your home seen on these sites? Ninety-five percent of all home buyers in the country say they first saw the home they bought online. Getting your home on the MLS is not an option. Failure to do so is to guarantee you won't get the best price in the least time.

A common complaint from people about bad real estate agents goes something like, "All my last agent did was to put a sign in my yard and put it on the MLS. Why should I give them three percent of the sale for that?" As complaints go, this one makes a strong point. If that's all they do, they aren't worth three percent! You could do this yourself, and in very strong seller's markets, it's an option worth exploring. Yet, if you can find an agent with a track record of getting more than three percent over average prices, why should you bother doing any of the work yourself?

What else can someone do besides the MLS to promote their house for sale? How about Facebook? I hear it's going to be huge with the kids.

Facebook is, right now, the single most effective, targeted, advertising platform available. Have a house near a major local employer? Do you know you can target ads to employees of that company? Is your house near a golf course? How about targeting people with golf as an interest? If you're looking to handle your house sale yourself, learn Facebook. There are more books and courses written on how to do this than I can mention, and the tech is changing with such speed that, if I bothered to go into more detail, it would be out dated by the time you read it here. Jot yourself a note to learn about it if you are going the For Sale By Owner route, as it is a great arrow to have in your marketing quiver.

The marketing you can avoid is any sort of print media. Buyers are not looking at print when they want to buy. Consider your own habits when you're shopping. Chances are excellent you're not looking at the newspaper for anything other than coupons (if even that).

When you see real estate ads in print media, those are placed by real estate agencies to attract your attention as a seller, not to attract buyers! They're playing into the *Availability Heuristic* and want you to think, "Wow, look at all their listings. They must be good. Let's use them when I want to sell." It's one way Realtors try to stay on the "top of mind." As far as promoting your house for sale, it's a waste of money.

Side Note: Advertising your house online, which is mandatory, requires photographs (duh) and, if you are using Facebook, video. Again, if you've hired an agent with a great track record, this is not something you need worry about as they'll be handling it. But if you are going on your own, spend the money needed on a good photographer. You can ask Realtor friends who they use, look at portfolios online, search the MLS for photos you like and call those agents to get the name of the photographer; any way you do it is fine. But don't cut corners here. Nothing will make your house sit on the market, unsold, quite like bad photos.

If you want a good laugh, Google "bad MLS photos." If it hasn't been obvious before, it will be obvious after you see these; not all Realtors are created equal.

Prospecting

Prospecting is very different from marketing. When you're marketing, you're sending out the message that your house is for sale and waiting for a response to come in. On the other hand, when you're prospecting, you're reaching out to potential buyers either by phone or in person. You are striking up a specific conversation, one on one: "Hey, this house is on the market. Are you interested in buying it or do you know anyone who might be?"

Marketing is a passive approach, and prospecting is a very active one. If you want to sell your house for the most money in the least amount of time, prospecting is a must!

I realize people generally hate prospecting. It's seems so salesy, so pushy. For the most part, people don't like talking to strangers; I know I don't. But if you're committed to selling a commodity in a crowded marketplace, you might want to suck it up and do what works.

Every person on my team spends 15 to 20 hours every week prospecting for buyers for our clients' properties. This includes calling on the phone and knocking on the doors of the neighbors to see if they know anyone who might be interested in living in the neighborhood. We usually target about 100 neighbors to door knock and about 1,000 to call.

You're no longer only stating that your house is on the market; you're now asking for interest. If you don't have the time or desire to prospect, I understand, but you aren't going to get the most money in the least amount of time. That's the trade-off.

Not every Realtor does a lot of active prospecting, but I'm willing to bet if you find one who sells homes for more than average, they do. This is not a real estate thing. This is a life thing – if you don't do *all* the work you can possibly do, especially the work you don't like, you don't get to expect *all* the results. Find an agent who gets better results and I bet you find someone who does the work others don't.

> **Key Point:** If you choose to sell your house on your own, and you want to get the most money in the least time, then you'll need to handle all the promotion yourself. Remember, you are the CEO. If you don't want to pay a salesperson, then you need to do that job yourself. Sales is a function of what you say, how you say it, and how many of the right people you say it to. You have a commodity to sell. You need to tell people about it. The more you tell, the better.

Last thoughts on the "For Sale By Owner" (FSBO) route as they pertain to marketing. As the CEO of a company that isn't hiring a salesperson, you need to manage the way the market perceives you.

There's a chance the market will see you taking on the challenge without a professional as a form of boot strapping. A sort of hard nose, pioneer, gritty, maybe even inspiring type of approach. If you effectively manage the story of why you're going it alone, you can turn it into a positive.

But most don't manage the story because most don't grasp that they're the CEO of a company selling a commodity in a crowded marketplace. Most people heading into the world of selling their properties do so with all the professionalism of running a yard sale. Literally. They use the same, red and white, $3.99 sign from Lowes that, instead of announcing a "YARD SALE" happens to say, "HOME FOR SALE BY OWNER."

This is a bad look.

Think about what this communicates: Why do people go to yard sales? Do they go to pay full retail price? Do they go for the safety of knowing that if, perchance, their purchase is not exactly what they thought, they'd have a solid legal recourse? Do they go for the extraordinary professionalism? No? But, then why do they go?

They go for the bargains. They go in hopes of getting a deal, and if they're lucky, a steal! They go to find the Van Gogh hidden in the garage.

Unless you want to sell your house to bargain hunters, don't make your house sale look like a yard sale. If you're doing this on your own, then you'd be best served by making it look as little like you are doing this on your own as possible. The ***Representativeness Heuristic*** plays both ways. If it fits their mental model of a yard sale, prospective buyers will treat it like a yard sale. They will expect a bargain, and, if they have an agent, someone who negotiates home sales as their livelihood, you'll be at a disadvantage in your goal of selling for the most money.

You're not planning on passing the savings you're expecting from going it alone through to the buyer, are you? If you're not (and why would you?), then what possible advantage does the buyer get from buying directly from you versus buying "retail" (i.e., an agent-sold home)?

The correct answer to that question is nothing. They get nothing from cutting out the middle man if you're not giving them a discount. This is why the math on FSBO deals so rarely pans out for the seller the way they expect.

The more you focus your marketing on the fact that this is a FSBO, the more predictable it is that the buyer will expect a discount. Make the marketing focus on the house, the neighborhood, anything but the fact that this is not being sold professionally. I'm not saying selling on your own is always a bad idea. What I am saying is that you will be fighting the buyers' mindset, and you need to know that upfront to have the deal work for you.

Whether you're on your own or you hire professional help, the strength of your promotion will go a long way to determine the success of your sale. Again, this is not a phenomenon limited to real estate. All businesses selling a commodity in a marketplace rely on their ability to reach consumers when they are looking to buy.

Avoid Being Shortchanged: Shortcuts to Watch For

- *Representativeness Heuristic:* This will work against you if you opt to place a "For Sale By Owner" sign in your yard. If it looks like a yard sale, buyers will treat it like a yard sale.
- *Representativeness* and *Confirmation Bias*: This can influence what kind of marketing you use. Find agents who are successful and use them or do what they do. What you think works and what actually works can be very different.
- *Availability Heuristic*: Print advertising is designed to keep Realtors' ads at the top of your mind. Don't waste your money doing the same. Buyers are not waiting for the newspaper to find out about your home.

Points to Remember

- Marketing includes getting the word out that your house is for sale. You want to be included on the MLS as well as other online advertising spaces.
- Professional photography and video are not optional.
- Consider advertising on sites like Facebook and targeting specific users in your geographic area.
- Prospecting is active and includes calling and knocking on doors to ask if neighbors know anyone who might be interested in buying. If you want all the results you must do all of the work (or pay someone else to do it).

Chapter Twenty:

Come on In

"Be so good they can't ignore you."

– Steve Martin

Now that either you, or your Realtor, have done all the right marketing and prospecting, there should be interest and potential buyers wanting to see your house. Let's talk about the best way to let them.

To Open or Not to Open

If you're using a Realtor, they may suggest having an open house. An open house provides one more opportunity for the public to see your house, and as a rule, I recommend them. Neighbors will come through to look, real estate agents will send their buyers to view on their own, people very early in their hunt will pop by, and people looking on their own will come through. Some agents think they're a waste of time and some swear by them. In my experience, if they're done correctly, which means more than a sign in the yard and a few on the corner, it can be a great way to build buzz.

Something people often don't realize is that open houses represent a decent source of potential business for the Realtor. They're not only looking for someone to buy the house they're holding open, they're looking for unrepresented buyers. Smart Realtors take advantage of the fact that people will almost always hire the first Realtor they talk to, so they park themselves at open houses as a way of putting themselves in front of people who are shopping for a home but don't yet have a Realtor representing them. I know agents whose entire business model is based on holding open houses and meeting buyers.

This, by the way, doesn't mean there is something nefarious going on. Because the agent is looking for more business is no reason you shouldn't have an open house. I mention this only because it's something you might not have known and, as the CEO, you need to understand what's happening in your business. In fact, I'd encourage you to look at it from the perspective that if the agent does get a significant amount of their own business from open houses, they're adept at attracting a lot of buyers thus increasing the likelihood of your open house attracting the person who will buy your home.

I almost always recommend my clients hold their home open at least the first weekend. To gain the most traction, a day or two before, we go prospecting by knocking on 100 doors in the neighborhood inviting people to the open house. Consider making it an event. How about having a BBQ or a wine and cheese affair? (Be sure to check your local regulations about serving alcohol though.) I've known Realtors who bring in a food truck and a bouncy house. The more buzz you can create, the better. The more people you can attract to the open house and the more it looks like it's in demand, the more money you're likely to get.

What you do, and how you do it, will depend on your interpretation of current market conditions. You can attend other open houses while you are in the early stages of deciding to sell and copy what works. A solid plan is what matters for a successful open house. If all you're going to do is put a sign in the yard and announce it to Zillow, then I don't see much value in it.

Regardless of whether you have open houses or not, you do need to make the house available to buyers. You'll need to have clear instructions either on the MLS or with your Realtor about when the house is available and unavailable. Think this through thoroughly before going to market. If you're using a Realtor, you don't need to be there when prospective buyers visit, and in fact, *you should not be there*. That might mean you only want it shown between certain hours or on certain days. Are there pets to consider? Kids to clean up after? Alarms to be turned on and off? Walk through all of these caveats with your agent, and they should be able to set it all up.

If you are going DIY, then you need some way to let the buyers in yourself. (A professional listing will use an electronic key box that can only be accessed by licensed and bonded agents and records who came in and when.) DIY sellers should let people in but then effectively disappear. Trust me, anybody intelligent enough to find your house knows the difference between a bathroom and a bedroom; they don't need your help. This is a common time for the *Endowment Effect* to take over. Proud owners feel the need to point out the minute details of the home they love. This is a bad approach. How much do you love shopping with a salesperson hanging all over you? Don't do it. Remember the mantra: "Nobody is looking to buy your home – they are looking to buy theirs."

> **Side Note:** Since you won't be there (either because you've left in the case of a professional sale or aren't hanging over the shoulder of a prospective buyer in a DIY sale), don't take any chances. Whether you're using an agent or not, secure any valuables or store them elsewhere during the time your house is on the market.

In addition to the house being empty of people (and pets, if possible), it should be as clean as clean can be. This means no clutter and no laundry lying around. Faucets and sinks should be wiped off every day. No one wants to see toothpaste residue in the bathroom sink or spots on the mirror. Furniture should always be dusted. You want buyers to look around and think, "Wow, I wish I lived here, it's so clean." In fact, you want to look around and think, "This house is great – I can't believe I'm leaving."

Scented candles and ionizers are helpful if you have pets or are a smoker, as clean needs to include odors as well. Get copies of *Architectural Digest* or *Dwell* and look at how those homes are presented. The more yours can look that clean, the more money you're likely to get.

Put it this way: A buyer may not notice how clean the house is, but I guarantee you, they'll notice dirt and clutter. You must be vigilant about cleaning up when your house is on the market and subject to a showing. Yes, this can be a tedious task, especially when there are kids and pets involved, but if you want the most money in the least time, you have to do it.

Since you want your house viewed as often as possible, and it can be a headache to have to continually clean up and leave, open houses make this easier – a lot of traffic in a concentrated period of time.

To go back for a moment, this is why pricing is so critical. Having an occupied house on the market for an extended period is an epic hassle, and having an unoccupied house sit on market unsold usually means extra expense. Pricing the house right will minimize the time on market (as will a well laid out marketing and prospecting campaign) and limit the expense and hassle of selling.

A critical, and often overlooked aspect of showing the house, is getting feedback. The feedback you receive from the market will come in two forms:

1. What people say with their mouths, and
2. What they say with their actions

Your agent should have systems in place to collect and provide you with feedback from the prospective buyers who visited the property. Selling on your own means you will need to create your own systems – ask people to sign a guest book, call people after they attend, talk to people on the way out, etc.

As the CEO, this feedback is crucial. It's real time market data. You need to look at the sales data to know what the market thinks. Watch for your own **Anchoring Heuristic** and **Confirmation Bias**. The market is talking, and that's the only conversation you should be listening to.

Don't get attached (**anchored**) to the price you set. At best, it was an educated guess. While we've been looking at your house like a commodity, it is also important to realize its uniqueness. Not only are the physical attributes of the property and its location unique, but the time in which it's selling is unique. Did another similar house come to market down the block priced 20 percent lower? In the time since you decided on your price, a lot could have happened. People get **anchored** to anything, and it's important for the showing/feedback stage that you treat your price as a "suggested" price. The market sets the price, not you.

I can't tell you the number of conversations I've had with sellers about how "If we found the right buyer, they'd surely pay the asking price." That's a CEO talking to themselves about how the market is wrong. That's what the **Endowment Effect** and **Confirmation Bias** sound like. People in the grips of those say things like, "I know what my house is worth!"

No. No you don't. The market knows what your house is worth. That's someone gripping onto their view of what "should" be happening and wishing the world would show up that way.

The market is never wrong. The people who came to see the house are the people you attracted with the price you promoted to them. You'd be better served right now to listen to what they're saying rather than to arguing that you haven't found "the one."

As a general rule of thumb, no showings in five consecutive days and/or no offers in seven days indicates your house is overpriced. The data unequivocally shows that houses sell for the most money the first two weeks they're on the market. This makes sense. When buyers walk into a house they ask first, "What's the price?" followed by "How long has it been on the market?" They know the longer it's on the market, the less competition they face and the higher likelihood that the seller is getting tired of selling. They rarely pay full price after the first week or two, and if it goes longer than a few weeks, buyers begin to think there's something wrong with the house and are willing to pay even less.

This live market data is information you can only get after showings begin. Everything up until now has been theory. Having potential buyers in your home is lab time. You're live – listen to what people are saying (with their mouths and their actions) and pivot accordingly.

Avoid Being Shortchanged: Shortcuts to Watch For

- *Endowment Effect*: Make sure this doesn't shape your showings to potential buyers. They are not buying your home, so you needn't hang all over them to tell them the tiny things you've loved about it.
- *Confirmation Bias* and *Anchoring*: These can shape your interpretation of what the market is saying as it goes through the process of making (or not making) offers on your house. Like it or not, the only opinion that matters is the market's, and it's during the showing phase that you'll learn what the market thinks. Everything up until now has been theory. This is live market data. Listen carefully.

Points to Remember

- For an open house to be as successful as possible, you should be prospecting and reaching out to about 100 of your neighbors beforehand.
- For showings after the open house, neither you nor your Realtor should be present (with rare exception).
- Secure your valuables for showings.
- Your house must be spotless, and I do mean spotless, without clutter around. It can be difficult to constantly keep the house clean and free of clutter and laundry, but it is mandatory if you want to get the most money in the least amount of time!
- No showings for five days and/or no offers in seven days indicate your house is likely overpriced.
- Houses sell for the most money the first week or two they're on the market and get less the longer they sit.

Chapter Twenty-one:

Deal or No Deal

"The most difficult thing in any negotiation, almost, is making sure that you strip it of the emotion and deal with the facts."
— *Howard Baker*

Whew! You've gone through the whole non-stop series of 30-minute parties for strangers called "showings." You've managed to keep the house clean for what could seem like a year and you've kept your mouth shut as people discuss the thing you love as if it were just a bunch of wood and brick. But now you have an offer – or better – multiple offers.

In a seller's market, if you set an offer review date and you did everything else right, you could have five or six offers to review. In a buyer's market, you might be happy to receive one. In either case, remember the faster you get an offer, the more money you stand to make for the house. By all measures, houses receive the most money in the first 14 days of being on the market.

Whether you have one or many, you must now do that which most Americans disdain. Negotiate. To say Americans don't like to haggle is like saying we don't like fried grasshoppers. We don't just **not like it** – we think it's sort of gross. Haggling is something other cultures do. It's why buying a car seems so unappealing, i.e., "What's it gonna take to get you into this house today?"

If you've taken the advice offered so far and hired representation with a track record of getting the most money in the least time, then you've likely found someone who negotiates well. If you are going it on your own and you want to get the most money, you better get prepared to negotiate.

In either case, you're still the CEO and you should learn the various components of the offer you'll receive. There's more to it than simply taking the highest offer. The sale of a home is unique and has unique conditions that are part of the sale.

When setting the house up for marketing, price was king; however now, when negotiating the sale, the highest price might not be the best offer. You'll need to understand how earnest money, down payment, funding source, closing date, closing costs, and contingencies all shape the strength of an offer. Even if you only have one offer, it's critical to understand all the aspects of it, so you don't get stuck holding the bag later.

It would be normal to wonder, "When is the highest price offer not the best offer?" My answer to that is: "When it's not." The point isn't to be offered the most money; the point is to get paid the most money. As you'll see, the time between being offered the money and being able to collect the money is tricky to navigate, and, given you don't do this very often, it's easy to miss things that will cost you in the end.

Much depends on your personal circumstances and what conditions the buyers are putting on the sale. For example, the highest-priced offer may come with a long-term closing date or be contingent on the buyer selling their current house. The highest offer might come from the buyer with the least attractive financing. You might want a rent-back while you go shopping for a house and the highest offer doesn't include one.

If you do get multiple offers and you are working on your own, you can download the spreadsheet/checklist of all the key areas you'll need to inspect at www.rationalrealestate.pro/offer If you're working with a Realtor, they should already have something like this. You'll want to make sure you've inspected and are clear about each of the touchpoints covered in detail in the next chapter.

If you do have multiple offers, now comes the fun part. Either you or your agent need to start calling all the offers you've received that are *not* your favorite and let them know they'll need to come up a bit (or a lot) to be considered. You're giving them a chance to offer again with their highest and best price. A couple may drop out at this point, but others will indeed come back with a revised offer.

You'll continue to do this – evaluate, pick your favorite, contact the remainder for another chance to raise their price – until everyone tells you that you have their highest and best. I've found that some people really don't like to go through this negotiation process. If you fall into this category, and truly want to get the most money for your house, you'll need to hire a Realtor who does enjoy this and is good at negotiating.

It's important to note that not all Realtors enjoy or do this process either. I've literally had agents tell me that they are expecting too many offers to be able to call through them so I should just submit my highest and best offer the first time. It breaks my heart for their client. That agent is absolutely leaving money on the table. In my view, it's a shocking disregard for her fiduciary responsibility to get her client the most money. Unfortunately, this is not uncommon. People often just refuse to do work they find distasteful and this is one more reason why, if you want the most money, looking at their personal track record of sold prices is critical.

If you only get one offer, and it's full price, hooray! However, if the single offer you receive is below your asking price, you'll have to go through some negotiating to see how close to your asking price you can get. This will depend on the market conditions and how much money you need to get out of the sale – in essence, your own bottom line.

Remember: The value of the house is what someone is willing to pay you to buy it *and* what it's worth to you to sell. As I shared at the beginning of this section, you might not *have* to sell your house. There may be a lot of reasons you *want* to sell, and, unfortunately, if you find yourself in a position in which you *must* sell, you're in the weakest negotiating position of all.

Here's where the *Anchoring Heuristic* can affect your ability to make a rational decision. For some people, once they've made up their mind to sell, that's it. That's their decision and their *anchor*. They become unwilling to stop the process and walk away even if they don't get the deal they want. If you really want to get the most you can for your house, you must have the mindset that you can walk away from the table and keep the house.

For successful negotiating, you need a "walk away point," and you should have that fixed in your mind. The "walk away point" is the point at which one dollar below this price, you will never sell the house. If you don't have this point clear in your mind, chances are good you'll wind up taking less than you could.

That said, it helps if you were realistic about the value of the house in the beginning. As I've said before, the *Endowment Effect, Anchoring*, and *Confirmation Bias* were all conspiring against you when you went to price the house. If you've let yourself fall victim to these shortcuts, I assure you, you'll either never sell your house (going through the expense and hassle of going to market for nothing) or you'll have a constant black cloud over your head about the sale price, forever grumbling that you didn't get enough for the house.

Avoid Being Shortchanged: Shortcuts to Watch For

- *The Anchoring Heuristic*: Don't let yourself become so *anchored* in the idea of selling that you are unwilling to walk away if you do not get the best or right offer for the house.

- ***The Endowment Effect***: Once again, and very bluntly, in all likelihood, the house is not worth what *you* think it is.
- ***Confirmation Bias***: It's too easy to fall victim to this shortcut, unless you come to terms with the fact that you don't set the price, only the market sets the price.

Points to Remember

- Create a spreadsheet on which to compare all the various factors of each offer including price, closing date, earnest money, and all other contingencies.
- Select your favorite offer, and then contact the others to give them the opportunity to raise their offer.
- Continue to evaluate/select/contact until you have it whittled down to the best offer.
- If you only get a single offer below your asking price, you can still negotiate to try to get the buyer closer to your price.
- You need to have a "walk away point," and you should be clear about this number before you put the house on the market.

Chapter Twenty-two:

Navigating the Sale to Closing – Stick the Landing

"The three great essentials to achieve anything worthwhile are: Hard work, Stick-to-itiveness, and Common Sense."
– Thomas A. Edison

You now have a great offer and a signed contract! Nice! What's next? While you might think the real work is over, there are still a few critical steps in the process before you can get your check and hand over the keys. Many of the particulars that follow will have been negotiated before you mutually agreed to the deal – and here is where you can see why each of those matters.

This, by the way, is the longest chapter in the selling section of this book. I'd like you to consider that this is indicative of how much there's still to accomplish. If you thought what came before was fun... just wait for this!

The shortcuts that tend to use people in this phase are of the "Oh, I didn't know to do that" variety, and as such, you should be wary of whatever reticence you have about asking questions of your legal team. If you've hired an agent, they should be handling everything that follows in this chapter. If you are going it alone, then it's up to whatever team you put together.

What follows is the basic outline of what a typical transaction will include, but be clear – every state, and city, is different, and there will likely be items required in your locale that are not covered in this chapter (or possibly things I've listed that aren't needed where you are).

More than just local laws are different and each contract is unique. For example, if the buyer needs to sell their home first, there are a whole slew of other steps to watch for; while if theirs is a cash offer to you, there will be fewer steps. All the more reason to use the questions outlined in the beginning of this book when interviewing agents. Remember – the agent you hire was required to study for 1/10 the time your barber was, and this is a lot more impactful than a haircut – do not assume your kid's soccer coach, or the "neighborhood expert," know what they're doing.

Every deal is different; although for you, it's all unique, which is why it's critical, if you're doing it without an agent, for you to be certain you have a good lawyer and/or escrow and title company on your team to see to it that all needed steps are handled with integrity.

Time is of the essence in this phase of the transaction as the contract you've signed has a closing date, and all the following steps, outlined in the contract, need to be completed, some in a specific order, on time for the deal to close. If any of these steps are not completed in the time specified in the contract, the deal can be voided and, worse, it's possible you could be liable for damages.

As the CEO, your job at this point is to make sure that all pieces are moving along. Your Realtor should manage this, or if you are going it alone, your escrow and legal team should manage it. But it's a good idea to know what's happening in your business at all times.

While your only real responsibility might look like it's monitoring and managing the timeline to ensure the buyer is taking the steps they need to take to get to closing, there are a lot of moving parts. If you're unaccustomed to handling these sorts of details, it can be a bit challenging. This is exactly where and how using a Realtor can pay off. Someone needs to keep the deal together if you want to get paid.

Given the serious nature of this, the fact that every deal is different, and it's the single largest financial contract you will likely face, do not take what follows as a comprehensive list of what you need to do. This is only a high-level overview of what you need to ask your legal team about.

Common steps to move from contract to close:

- Earnest money must be delivered to escrow.
- Accurate and clear title must be provided.
- Inspection contingency needs to be met and waived.
- Appraisal must be completed and value must at least match the agreed price.
- Loan must be approved through underwriting.
- Any locally required inspections must be completed.
- All documents must be delivered to each party and signed.
- House must be maintained, and cleaned per contract specs, prior to closing.
- Loan must be funded.
- Title must be recorded with the county.

Here's a quick overview of each of these steps:

Escrow

The purpose of escrow is to provide a neutral third party that collects documents from each side, assuring that each piece meets local standards. In some parts of the country, an LPO (limited practice office) or escrow office handles these duties, and in other locations, it's handled by a real estate attorney. They will generally be the ones to hold the buyer's earnest money deposit in their account to assure the buyer performs as agreed. The earnest money is released back to the buyer at the conclusion of the contract (usually to be used as down payment or to cover their closing costs). Should the buyer fail to perform, that money goes to the seller.

> **Side Note:** There'd almost always be some huge legal fight for the buyer to forfeit their earnest money. I am sure it happens, but I've never personally seen it. I try my best to stay away from huge legal fights... they rarely turn out well for anyone but the lawyers. In other words, as the seller, while the amount of earnest money shows the financial solvency and commitment the buyer has, it would be a rare occasion in which the deal would go so far south that you would get to keep the money and then sell the house to someone else.

Title

The title company is, in essence, a very niche insurance company. They only sell title insurance. That is, they are willing to extend a policy that assures the buyer, and their lender, that you, the seller, have legal authority to sell the property. The title outlines any liens, easements, or other restrictions there are on the use or sale of the land. The title company will have researched the history of the title and will provide documentation that each side should inspect to make certain the sale covers what you expect it to cover.

Remember: You get what you *inspect* not what you *expect*. Take the time to read and understand the title. It outlines exactly what you are selling. Any title company will be happy to take the time to explain how to read your title, as would any reputable and educated Realtor. Take advantage of that opportunity.

Depending on market conditions, either the buyer or the seller will be the first to suggest the title/escrow company (in a buyer's market, it's the buyer, and in a seller's market, it's the seller). This is generally not a big deal, and I would never waste a negotiating "chip" on title/escrow company selection. If the other side wants someone in particular, I wouldn't make a big fuss unless you have reason to doubt the competency or honesty of their preference.

Inspection

If you agreed to price and terms and your contract is contingent on a home inspection by the buyer, they'll be doing one now. Regardless of whether you said the house is being sold "as is" or not, the inspection contingency allows them to inspect the house, and should they not like what it says, for any reason at all, the contingency almost always allows them to get out of the deal and get their earnest money returned. You'll need to read the contingency included from the buyer to be clear as to what rights it gives them as the standard versions differ from state to state.

An inspection contingency is usually something of a "get out of deal free" card for the buyer. As such, this almost always opens a second round of negotiations as the buyer would be foolish to not at least ask for some repairs. Why wouldn't they? They have all the leverage at this point. Your house is now off the market, and if the deal falls through, you'll need to go back through all the showings and marketing again. Plus, you'll need to disclose to any new buyer anything the inspection revealed that you hadn't known about previously. It's a mess.

This second negotiation is something a lot of sellers don't think through before the sale. The weakened negotiating position for you as the seller alone is enough for me to strongly suggest to my clients that they do the inspection before listing. If you've followed my advice from Chapter 18 and included the pre-inspection as part of your prep work prior to sale, this won't be an issue. You'll have given the inspection to all the prospective buyers, and even if, for some reason, you've allowed for an inspection contingency, you and the buyer will at least be as clear as possible about what they are buying. Having the inspection done up front almost always eliminates the problems in this phase.

As I'm writing this, I'm representing two different buyers in transactions in which, had the seller done the inspection report up front and provided it to us, we would have accepted the condition of the house and offered the same amount. As it is, with our having a contingency that allows us to exit the deal should we not like what we see in the report, we are receiving over $5,000 off the sale price. Because the seller tried to save $500 up front, it is literally costing them $5,000. You do the math.

After the inspection (that essentially protects the buyer), there will be, if a lender is providing the funding, an appraisal to protect the lender. This is distinct from the inspection, and the lender should never, under any circumstances, see the inspection report. They do not need it, they won't ask for it, and if for some reason they get a copy, it will create massive headaches for you. Again, it's rare that this happens, but you do need to understand this, so you don't make a mistake. The potential problem you're out to avoid is having the underwriting department see the report and demand some repair prior to funding the loan. Yes, it's a little silly. They know there was an inspection completed and they know they don't have the report, so they agree to proceed as if everything is fine. Odd as that seems, that is the current system, and all you need to do is make sure you don't send anything about the inspection to the lender. Enough said.

Appraisal

The appraisal is ordered and paid for by the buyer and is something over which you have little control. If you are going it alone, you want to make certain that the buyer and their agent moves this along in a timely manner. It could take a week, or more, for the appraiser to get to you and view the property and another week for them to submit their report. If the inspection took a week to resolve, you're now at least three weeks in and the lender hasn't even started the final paperwork. Making sure this moves along is critical, so don't assume anything. Stay in communication with your agent, or if you don't have one, the buyer's agent.

There is always a chance the home won't appraise for the amount offered, and the odds of this happening increase as you go higher and higher over the list price. In a hot seller's market, it's not unheard of for houses to go for 10 to 20 percent over the asking price (my personal best is 37 percent over asking... *THAT* was fun). This sometimes creates a problem when the lender cannot find similar, comparable homes (comps) to justify the sale price. In that case, the lender will only lend on the amount they feel the house could be sold for, based on the comps. This means the buyer will either need to make up the difference or negotiate with you to lower the price.

The best-case scenario here is to address this in the original negotiation. If you hired, or are, a strong negotiator and there were offers over asking price, you should have had at least some opportunity to demand the buyer add additional down payment should the appraisal not meet the sale price. Adding additional down payment effectively lowers what is needed from the lender, thus compensating for the lower than expected appraisal. As discussed earlier, the highest price offer is not always the strongest one for this very reason.

One sort of cool secret is that you can sometimes supply comps yourself to help justify the sale price. If I ever have a question of the house appraising for the sale price, I go through the MLS and pick comps that justify the price I want and leave them for the appraiser. There's nothing unethical about this. The current rules prohibit the lender from influencing the appraiser – there is nothing preventing the Realtor from speaking with them. You'll just be making certain the appraiser doesn't miss anything, and they'll often thank you for doing the work. Of course, sometimes they don't want your comps, but it never hurts to ask. Make sure you or your agent is ready to do this as it can be a deal saver.

There's a much bigger problem that a low appraisal has, and most people never deal with it. If the loan is FHA insured, then the low appraisal will "stick" to the house for six months. That is, if the offer you accepted is using an FHA-guaranteed loan to buy the house, the appraisal value will be on file for the house for six months. This means, in essence, that if the appraisal is low, you'll most likely need to lower your price to that value regardless of what you agreed to. Why? Because if you don't, the buyer could walk away, and now, when you find a new buyer, their bank will see the appraised value you just received. Your house now has a value associated with it, and anyone using an FHA loan will see that. What would the motivation of the next buyer be to offer you more than that? There isn't one... and they won't.

This is why the financing terms of the offer you accept are critical and why the highest price is not always the best offer. It is also why you would be best served by assembling a team of professionals behind you. Rules and regulations are constantly changing, and unless selling houses is something you do all the time, the chance of you getting caught in an untenable situation because of something of which you were unaware is fairly high. Don't cut corners on your team.

Underwriting

As far as I'm concerned, this is the ultimate black box in the deal. Underwriting is the process by which the lender inspects all the information they have about the house and the borrower and gives the thumbs up to release the money the buyer offered you. Underwriters protect the lender. You'll never meet the underwriter. It's they who control the transaction, and it's why it's critical to the deal that the buyer picks a lending institution with a track record of closing on time.

You have no control over what actions the buyer takes between signing with you and the time the deal closes. If you've had an inspection and appraisal, you could be three weeks into the transaction already. The underwriter might not even get started with the paperwork until this point. If something changed in the buyer's credit (say, they bought a car... which happens sometimes), this could easily sour the deal. And there's nothing you can do about it! All the more reason why you need to take the time to vet each offer and their lender. I'll say it one more time: This is a piece of the process during which having professional help on your side can save you money by avoiding pitfalls you might not otherwise recognize.

The big banks (pick any one for this) have their underwriters sitting somewhere across the country, unreachable by the person representing the buyer. This is why, again, I recommend you only accept an offer from a local lender or broker that specializes in home loans. That is, pick someone who can walk across the hall, sit down with the underwriter, talk to them, and get the deal moving should it get stuck. This won't happen with a big bank. If you have any leverage in the negotiation, I'd trade a bit of price for a more reliable close every day.

You can, by the way, ask that a buyer be pre-approved by your lender before you will accept their offer. You cannot demand that they switch lenders, but if they are pre-approved by your person, and their own team falters, jeopardizing the deal, you could, at that time, ask them to switch to keep the deal alive.

Signing and Closing

Once the loan has cleared underwriting, they will release the documents to the escrow company. Once escrow gets these documents, they'll draw up the Closing Disclosure Documents. This is a five-page document that the buyer receives that shows the buyer the exact costs of the loan and allows them to compare everything to the estimate they received when they applied for the loan. There is a mandatory, three-business-day window between this document being released and when the buyer can sign for the loan. This makes the timing of document release by underwriting critical. If you've had inspections and appraisals, and underwriting is slow, you can run into issues with closing on time if not tightly managed.

Escrow will call you to come in to sign your closing documents. Different states handle this differently, so check with your team about the process where you live. If you're out of town, often they can send a mobile notary and have you sign wherever you happen to be. This is not a casual, "one document, sign here" type of thing. There will be dozens of legal documents and your team can explain each one as you sign. Have I mentioned that you shouldn't skimp on hiring a team here?

After both parties have signed all the documents, they go back to the lender for final approval. They check everything over one more time to make sure every "i" is dotted, every "t" is crossed, and (fingers crossed) release the funds to escrow.

Before funds are released, a buyer will often ask to do a final walk through to make certain that you have cleaned the house, and it's in the same condition as when they wrote the offer. After all, it could be a month since they've seen it and a lot could've happened during that time. This is quite normal, and I'd count on them asking you to do this. It is possible that if they don't like what they see, they can instruct their lender to not release the funds, delay closing, cancel the deal, or in some way create a problem. Read your contract, and the buyer, carefully. Learn what is expected and deliver the product the customer wants. Remember, you are the CEO of a company selling a commodity right up until the end.

Once the bank turns over the money to escrow, they'll release the title to record with the county and disperse the funds, paying off all parties in the process. They'll pay things like utilities, taxes, Realtor commissions, their own fees, lender fees, etc. and then cut you a check for the remainder. They can send that to you in the mail, you can pick it up, or they can direct deposit it – you'd work that out with them before closing.

The deed should record with the county the day they release it, and you should get paid the next business day. Again, every locality is different, so ask well ahead of time about the specifics for where you live.

Once the deed is recorded, the other agent, or you if this was done entirely DIY, will hand over the keys to the buyer and transaction is complete.

So... did you stick the landing? Congrats.

Avoid Being Shortchanged: Shortcuts to Watch For

The shortcuts that occur in this part of the process are of the "I didn't know I was supposed to do that" type. The problem is one of mindset, and no one wants to look stupid, so they don't open their mouth and ask. This is the worst possible time for you to fall victim to that.

Points to Remember

- If you are handling the sale on your own, hire an escrow/title company or an attorney. If you have an agent, they will have these connections.
- Ensure that the agreed-upon earnest money is deposited into escrow.
- Whether or not an inspection was done prior to listing and offers, the buyer may ask to do one themselves. Even if you insisted that you wouldn't

make any further repairs or changes, be prepared –
the buyer might ask anyway!

- Your responsibility at this point is to continue to
  shepherd the deal toward closing and monitor the
  timeline to ensure that the buyer's tasks (inspection, appraisal, etc.) are being done according to
  their deadlines.
- Never think that the deal is done when you sign
  the contract. The time between contract and closing
  can be tenuous and a lot can go wrong. The deal is
  done when you are handed the check.

Chapter Twenty-three:

SOLD!

"I may not have gone where I intended to go, but I think I have ended up where I intended to be."

– Douglas Adams

Whether you are buying or selling, getting the keys or the check, respectively, completes the process. You now either own a house or sold your home.

My hope is that by educating yourself not only on the real estate transaction process but – and possibly most importantly – on the psychological shortcuts that plague us all, you now own your dream home and/or got the most money in the least amount of time for the house you sold.

That has certainly been my personal goal in writing this book. There is only an infinitesimal chance that I can act as your Realtor. Regardless, I wanted to share the problems I've seen crop up time and time again that I attribute to the shortcuts we've covered throughout this book.

I cannot overstate the importance of interviewing the real estate agent who will represent you on either side of the transaction – the one that involves the most expensive and most impactful thing you will ever buy or sell. With what I've shared, you should now have a much clearer insight about how the industry works and how truly insane it is to select an agent because they were the first one you met at an open house, came to you as a referral from your wife's best friend's cousin's husband, or they had a good profile on the internet.

I hope you are now fully empowered to move much more effectively and successfully through whatever real estate transaction you face – buying, selling, or both – and the result leads to many happy years and memories.

Resources:

For convenience, here are the links that have been referenced throughout the book:

- www.rationalrealestate.pro/246: From Chapter 2, watch the video of the experiment on **_Confirmation Bias_** in which students were asked to develop an hypothesis about the sequence "2,4,6" and determine what the rule actually was. The true rule is shared at the end of the video.
- www.rationalrealestate.pro/interview: From Chapter 6: Download an editable version of the pre-interview email that you can customize and send to real estate agents you are interested in interviewing.
- www.rationalrealestate.pro/null: From Chapter 9: Download this list of all of a property's shortcomings along with the opportunity to list any deficiency as curable or incurable for any property on which you are considering placing an offer.
- www.rationalrealestate.pro/video: From Chapter 10: Find training videos that cover some of the most common aspects of writing an offer.
- www.rationalrealestate.pro/inspection: From Chapter 12: Find a sample inspection report that will show you the level of detail that these reports typically cover.
- www.rationalrealestate.pro/offers: From Chapter 21: Download this spreadsheet/checklist to help you compare offers you receive that covers all of the key areas to review in order to determine the best offer.

About the Author

Aaron Hendon is a Seattle Realtor, real estate investor, entrepreneur, educator, and national speaker. He is managing partner of Christine & Company, a *Seattle Magazine*-awarded Five Star Real Estate Agent winning team, 2012-2017. He is also an individual recipient of the Rising Star of Seattle Real Estate award in 2016 and a personal winner of the Five Star Professional Award in 2017.

Author of *Don't Get Fooled Again: An Insider's Guide to the Seven Questions You Must Ask to Avoid Hiring the Wrong Real Estate Agent (again)*, and *All Realtors are Not Created Equal*, Aaron has been actively educating people to make smarter choices for over 20 years. He has lead transformational educational seminars and leadership development programs for thousands of people nationally since 1995.

Born in New York, Aaron graduated SUNY Purchase with a BFA in 1987. Realizing his art degree made him eligible to work in food service anywhere in the country he followed his girlfriend to NM and promptly started waiting tables. In 1990, he opened a real New York bagel shop in Albuquerque, selling it nine years later as a business grossing over $1,000,000 annually.

Eventually landing in Northwest in 2000, he now lives on a small island off the coast of Seattle with his brilliant wife, Kael, his two brilliant children, Leela (14) and Jonah (11), and his adoring, if not exactly brilliant, Golden Doodle, Rozy.

Contact Aaron:

aaron@rationalrealestate.pro
206-280-3312
1307 N 45th St.   Ste 300
Seattle, WA 98103

Made in the USA
Middletown, DE
12 April 2018